My
CROCHET
WARDROBE

CASSIE WARD

Tuva Publishing

www.tuvapublishing.com

Address Merkez Mah. Cavusbasi Cad. No:71
Cekmekoy - Istanbul 34782 / Turkey
Tel: +9 0216 642 62 62

My Crochet Wardrobe

First Print 2019 / December

All Global Copyrights Belong To
Tuva Tekstil ve Yayıncılık Ltd.

Content Crochet

Editor in Chief Ayhan DEMİRPEHLİVAN

Project Editor Kader DEMİRPEHLİVAN

Designer Cassie WARD

Technical Editors Rachel VOWLES, Leyla ARAS, Büşra ESER

Graphic Designers Ömer ALP, Abdullah BAYRAKÇI, Zilal ÖNEL

Photograph Tuva Publishing

ISBN 978-605-7834-07-2

Contents

Projects

Introduction

As a child I was always creative. I could draw, paint, sew, knit and embroider. My great Aunt Alice was an avid crocheter and I longed to be able to do what she did. I'm left handed and after many unsuccessful attempts to teach me, she finally gave up on me.

After the tragedy of losing my dear mum Josie in my late 20's, I suffered terribly with anxiety and needed a distraction from my overactive mind. I was at an exhibition sitting next to a lovely Irish lady from the UK Hand Knitting Association. I picked up a hook, she taught me the basics of crochet there and then and sent me on my way. I was instantly addicted and began designing immediately.

I made amazing creations, but never having learned how to read a pattern, I had no real idea of what stitches I was using! I needed proper lessons. I heard of a very lovely lady named Helen who taught me how to read patterns and showed me new techniques. From this, The Missing Yarn was born.

I love playing with different stitches, styles and textures. Many of my designs are born out of my love of fashion and desire to be different. My designs have appeared in Inside Crochet, Crochet Now, Simply Crochet, Mollie Makes and the Crochet Society Box. You can find more of my patterns at www.themissingyarn.co.uk

When I'm not crocheting, I'm a single mum to the most amazing identical twin boys whose drive and determination to succeed amazes me on a daily basis. I'm so proud of the young men they are becoming. We live in a sleepy English village in Cambridgeshire with our little dog Coco.

This book is an absolute dream come true and I'm so thankful for the opportunity to share my designs with you. I hope the book will inspire you to make some beautiful, unique crochet garments and that you get the same amount of joy from making them it as I did from writing them.

Cassie

Cambridgeshire 2019

p.18

p.26

p.32

p.38

p.42

p.48

p.54

p.58

p.62

p.66

p.72

p.76

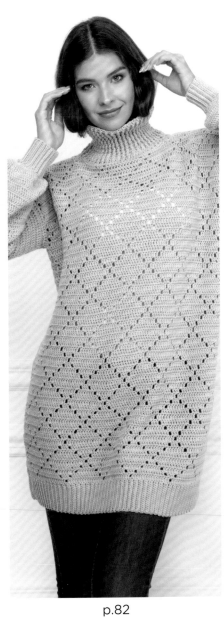

p.82

p.88

p.92

YARNS AND MATERIALS

There are many choices of yarn you can use for making garments. Throughout this book Scheepjes Yarns are used. If you wish to make your garment in a different yarn there are three important things to be considered. Firstly be sure that the substitute yarn works to the same tension as stated in the pattern otherwise your garment could end up being larger or smaller than the given size. Secondly, choose a yarn with a similar fibre content as this can affect the finished drape of the fabric. Finally check the ball yardage, and be sure to buy enough yarn so that you are able to complete the project without running out! To do this, multiply the number of balls needed for your size by the yardage of the stated yarn, this will give you the total yardage needed to make the garment. You can then work out how many balls to buy in your substitute yarn by dividing this number by the yardage of the substitute yarn ball.

Scheepjes Stone Washed XL

Fibre content: 70% Cotton, 30% Acrylic
Yarn Weight: Aran
Ball Weight: 50g
Length: 75m/82yds

Scheepjes Eliza

Fibre content: 100% Polyester
Yarn Weight: DK
Ball Weight: 100g
Length: 230m/252yds

Scheepjes Bloom

Fibre content: 100% Cotton
Yarn Weight: Aran
Ball Weight: 50g
Length: 80m/87yds

Scheepjes Merino Soft

Fibre content: 50% Wool Superwash Merino, 25% Microfiber, 25% Acrylic
Yarn Weight: DK
Ball Weight: 50g
Length: 105m/114yds

Scheepjes Whirligigette

Fibre content: 80% Virgin Wool, 20% Alpaca
Yarn Weight: DK
Ball Weight: 100g
Length: 215m/235yds

Scheepjes Stone Washed

Fibre content: 78% Cotton, 22% Acrylic
Yarn Weight: DK
Ball Weight: 50g
Length: 130m/142yds

Scheepjes Skies Heavy

Fibre content: 100% Premium Blend Cotton
Yarn Weight: DK
Ball Weight: 100g
Length: 170m/186yds

Scheepjes Catona Denim

Fibre content: Catona Denim 100% Cotton
Yarn Weight: 4ply
Ball Weight 50g
Length: 125m/136yds

Scheepjes Chunky Monkey Anti Piling

Fibre content: 100% Premium Acrylic
Yarn Weight: Aran
Ball Weight: 100g
Length: 116m/127yds

HOOKS

Always use the hook size given in the pattern. It is essential to work a tension swatch to ensure that your tension is correct and that your finished garment will measure the correct size. If you find you have more stitches in your swatch than the stated tension, use a larger hook, if you have fewer stitches then use a smaller hook.

	USA	English	Metric
	14	6	0.60
	12	5	0.75
	10	4	1.00
	-	3	1.25
	6	2.5	1.50
	4	2	1.75
	B	14	2.00
	C	12	2.50
	D	11	3.00
	E	9	3.50
	F	8	4.00
	G	7	4.50
	H	6	5.00
	I	5	5.50
	J	4	6.00
	K	2	7.00
	-	1/0	8.00
	-	2/0	9.00
	P	3/0	10.00

Tension

Crochet Tension is the number of stitches and rows, using a certain stitch or stitch pattern in a defined square of crochet. In this book we have used 10cm x 10cm (4in x 4 in). It is determined by the size of hook and yarn you are using .

The tension required for each pattern is listed in the information section of the patterns, you need to work to the stated tension to ensure that your garment turns out to be the correct size.

It is essential therefore to check your tension before you start by making a tension square.

At tension square should be slightly larger than the area you are going to measure.
When you have made your tension square measure the stitches on a flat surface.

If you have too many stitches then your tension is too tight, if you have too few stitches then your tension is too loose.

You may need to work up a few tension squares with different hook sizes to achieve the correct tension to match the pattern.

Joining Methods

There are two main ways I use to join my crochet garments. You really can use whichever method suits you, some people find it easier to sew using a large darning needle and others prefer to crochet the seams together. For the patterns in this book you can use either method for any garment.

If sewing, use whip stitch, if crocheting, use single crochet. There are many excellent on line tutorials for this. Some top tips are always align the pieces and pin in the exact position you wish to join them.

Always join with the right sides together so you get the seam on the inside of your garments, work through both loops of the stitches unless stated, using either method.

Blocking the garment

When you block crochet you are forcing your completed garment to dry in a certain position. Blocking is imperative to achieve a good finish to the garment.

Use a blocking matt, mist the garment with a spray of water until damp, lay and shape the pieces on your blocking matt and place little pins around the garment to hold it in shape, leave to dry on the blocking board. Only remove the garment when it's totally dry.

Weaving in ends

When you have finished your garment it's essential you weave in ends correctly if you want your piece to last a long time and look neat.

Whilst weaving in ends doesn't take a lot of time or concentration, you do need to do it correctly so that your crochet doesn't unravel and so the ends don't poke out.

Using a tapestry needle run the needle through a couple of stitches, change directions and run it vertically then weave it in the opposite direction, going up and down and side to side will help to lock the stitch in.

Remember to always weave stitches on the wrong side of garment.

CROCHET STITCHES

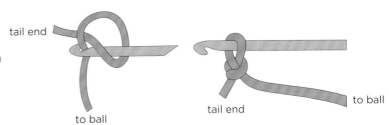

Slip Knot

Make a loop with your yarn, insert the hook through the loop and pick up the ball end of the yarn, draw through loop and pull in tail end gently.

Yarn Round Hook (yrh)

Wrap the yarn from back to front around your hook.

Chain (ch)

Start with a slip knot or loop on the hook, *yrh and pull through the loop on your hook*. To work more chain stitches repeat from * to *.

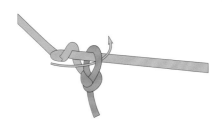

Single Crochet (sc)

Insert hook into stitch or space indicated, yrh and draw up a loop, (2 loops on hook), yrh and pull through both loops to complete the stitch.

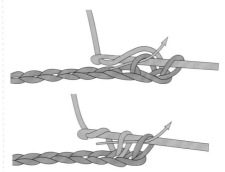

Half Double Crochet (hdc)

Yrh, insert hook into stitch or space indicated, yrh and draw up a loop, (3 loops on hook), yrh and draw through all three loops to complete the stitch.

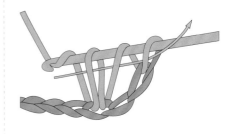

Double Crochet (dc)

Yrh, insert hook into stitch or space indicated, yrh and draw up a loop (3 loops on hook), yrh and draw through two loops, yrh and draw through next two loops to complete the stitch.

Treble Crochet (tr)

Wrap yarn twice around hook, insert hook into stitch or space indicated, yrh and draw up a loop, (4 loops on hook), *yrh and draw through 2 loops; repeat from * twice more to complete the stitch.

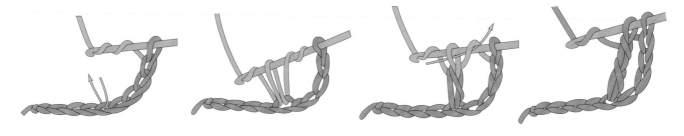

Slip Stitch (sl st)

Insert hook into stitch or space indicated, yrh and draw up a loop, pull this new loop through the loop on your hook to complete the stitch.

Double Crochet Two Together (dc2tog)

Yrh, insert hook into stitch, yrh and draw up a loop, (3 loops on hook), yrh, pull through two loops, (2 loops on hook), yrh, insert hook into next stitch, yrh and draw up a loop, (4 loops on hook), yrh and pull through two loops, (3 loops on hook), yrh and pull through remaining three loops.

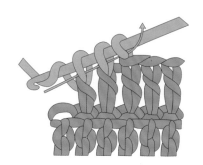

Double Crochet Seven Together (dc7tog)

*Yrh, insert hook into next stitch, yrh and draw up a loop, (3 loops on hook), yrh, pull through two loops, (2 loops on hook); repeat from * a further six times over next six stitches, yrh and pull through remaining loops.

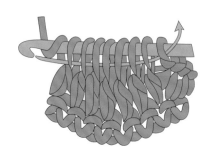

Front Post Double Crochet (fpdc)

Yrh, insert hook from front to back to front around vertical post of next stitch, yrh and draw up a loop, (3 loops on hook), yrh and draw through two loops, yrh and draw through next two loops to complete the stitch.

Back Post Double Crochet (bpdc)

Yrh, insert hook from back to front to back around vertical post of next stitch, yrh and draw up a loop, (3 loops on hook), Yrh and draw through two loops, yrh and draw through next two loops to complete the stitch.

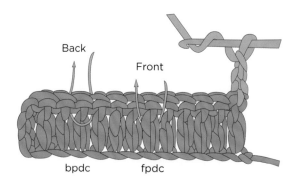

Back Post Double Crochet Four Together (bpdc4tog)

*Yrh, insert hook from back to front to back around vertical post of next stitch, yrh and draw up a loop, (3 loops on hook), Yrh and draw through two loops; repeat from * a further three times, yrh and pull through remaining loops.

Back Post Double Crochet Seven Together (bpdc7tog)

*Yrh, insert hook from back to front to back around vertical post of next stitch, yrh and draw up a loop, (3 loops on hook), Yrh and draw through two loops; repeat from * a further six times, yrh and pull through remaining loops.

Back Loop Only (blo)

Insert hook into back part of stitch only (ie the back part of the 'V" looking down on the stitch from the top.

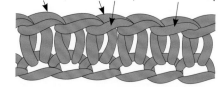

Loop Stitch (Lp St)

Working from the wrong side, wrap yarn from back to front around and over the index finger, holding the yarn (pull out a loop approx 4cm/1½in long), insert hook in next stitch, grab the yarn from behind and draw yarn through the stitch. With the loop still on your finger, yrh, and draw through both loops on hook

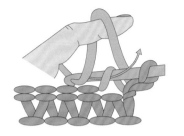 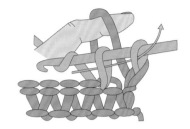 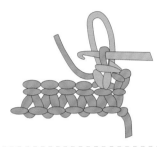

Cluster (Cl)

*Yrh, insert hook in stitch or space indicate, yrh draw loop through, yrh, draw through 2 loops; repeat from * four more times all in same st, yrh draw through all loops on hook.

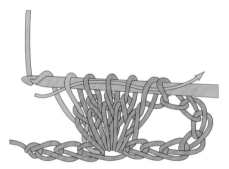 

Puff

*Yrh, insert hook in stitch or space indicated, yrh and pull up a loop to height of 1 dc; repeat from * twice more, (7 loops on hook), yrh, pull through all 7 loops, ch1 to close.

Beginning Puff (BegPuff)

Ch3, *yrh, insert hook in stitch or space indicated, yrh and pull up a loop to height of 1 dc stitch; repeat from * once more (5 loops on hook), yrh, pull through all 5 loops, ch1 to close.

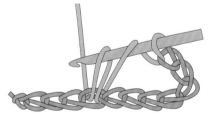 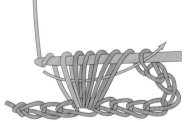

Fat Puff (FP)

*Yrh, insert hook, yrh, pull loop through to height of 1 dc; rep from * four more times, (11 loops on hook), yrh and pull through all 11 loops, 1ch to secure.

Shell

Shells are formed by working the given number of stitches into the same stitch or space.

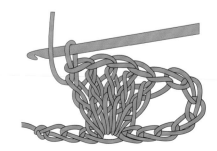

PROJECTS

Bobble Top
JUMPER

Bobble Top
JUMPER

Who doesn't love snuggling up by the fire in their favorite
jumper on a cold winter's night?
This jumper is perfect for cosy nights in or exploring the
wilderness on chilly days.

DIFFICULTY

★ ★ ★

MATERIALS

**Scheepjes Stone Washed XL, 70% cotton, 30% acrylic,
50g/75m/82yds**
Larimar 868 x 19 (20, 23, 26) balls
USJ-9/5.5mm and USJ-10/6mm hooks

YARN ALTERNATIVES

You can use any Aran weight yarn that works to the same
tension.

TENSION

Lower body: Work 14 sts and 11 rows in pattern to measure
10 x 10cm/4 x 4in using USJ-10/6mm hook.

Upper body: Work 14 sts and 10 rows in pattern to measure
10 x 10cm/4 x 4in using USJ-9/5.5mm hook.

SPECIAL STITCHES

Cluster (Cl): (Yrh, insert hook, yrh draw loop through, yrh,
draw through 2 loops) 5 times in next st, yrh draw through
all loops on hook.

MEASUREMENTS

SIZE	S	M	L	XL
Actual bust				
	91.5	100	108.5	117 cm
	36	39	42¾	46 in
Shoulder to shoulder				
	46	50	54	58 cm
	18	19½	21¼	23 in
Length to underarm				
	48	48	52	52 cm
	19	19	20½	20½ in

PATTERN STARTS

FRONT

WELT

Using USJ-9/5.5mm hook, ch12.
Row 1: 1sc in 2nd ch from hook and in each ch to end, turn - 11sc.
Rows 2-64 (70, 76, 82): Ch1, sc blo in each st to end, turn. Fasten off.
Turn work and evenly distribute 64 (70, 76, 82)sc along long edge of ribbed welt, turn.
Change to USJ-10/6mm hook.

Work in Lower Body Pattern as follows:

Row 1: Ch3, (counts as 1dc here and throughout), [1sc, 1dc] to last st, 1sc in last st, turn.
Row 2: Ch3, [1sc in next dc, 1dc in next sc] to last st, 1sc in 3rd of 3 ch, turn.
Rows 3-36 (36, 40, 40): Rep rows 1-2.

Continue in Upper Body Pattern as follows:

Row 1 (WS): Ch3, 1dc in each st to end, turn – 64 (70, 76, 82)dc.
Row 2 (RS): Ch1 (does not count as st here and throughout) 4sc, [1Cl (see Special Stitches), 5sc] to end turn.
Row 3: Ch3 (counts as 1dc), 1dc in each sc and Cl along row, turn.
Row 4: Ch1, 7sc, [1Cl, 5sc] to last 8 sts, 8sc, turn.
Change to USJ-9/5.5mm hook.
Row 5: Rep row 1.
Rows 6-21: Rep rows 2-5.**

SHAPE LEFT NECK

Row 22 (RS): Ch1, 4sc, [1Cl, 5sc] three times, 1Cl, 23 (23, 23, 29)sc, [1Cl, 5sc] three times, turn.
Row 23 (WS): Ch3, 24 (27, 30, 30)dc, dc2tog, turn - 26 (29, 32, 32) sts.
Row 24: Ch1, 5 (2, 5, 5)sc, [1Cl, 5sc] 3 (4, 4, 4) times, 3sc, turn.
Row 25: Ch3, 23 (26, 29, 29)dc, dc2tog, turn – 25 (28, 31, 31) sts.

Sizes S and M only

Row 26: Ch1, 7 (4)sc, [1Cl, 5sc] 3 (4) times, turn.
Row 27: Ch1, 4sc, 1hdc, 1dc in top of cl, 17 (20)dc, dc2tog, turn - 24 (27) sts.
Row 28: Ch1, 3 (6)sc, 1cl, 5sc, 1cl, 9sc, turn - 19 (22) sts.
Row 29: Ch1, 4sc, 2hdc, 11 (14)dc, dc2tog – 18 (21) sts.

Sizes L and XL only

Row 26: Ch1, 1sc, [1Cl, 5sc] 5 times, turn.

Row 27: Ch1, 4sc, 1dc, 1dc in top of cl, 23dc, dc2tog, turn - 30 sts.
Row 28: Ch1, 3sc, [1cl, 5sc] twice, 1cl, 9sc, turn – 25 sts.
Row 29: Ch1, 4sc, 2hdc, 17dc, dc2tog – 24 sts.

All sizes

Fasten off.

SHAPE RIGHT NECK

With WS facing, count in 27 (30, 33, 33) sts from side edge and rejoin yarn.
Row 23 (WS): Dc2tog, dc to end, turn - 26 (29, 32, 32) sts.

Sizes S and M only

Row 24: Ch1, 7sc, [1Cl, 5sc] twice, 1Cl, 6 (9)sc, turn.
Row 25: Dc2tog, dc to end, turn - 25 (28) sts.
Row 26: Ch1, 4sc, 1Cl, [5sc, 1cl] three times, 2 (5)sc, turn.
Row 27: Dc2tog, dc to last 5 sts, 1hdc, 4sc, turn, fasten off - 24 (27) sts.
Row 28: Miss 4sc and 1hdc and rejoin yarn in top of next st, 8sc, 1Cl, 5sc, 1Cl, 4 (7)sc, turn - 19 (22) sts.
Row 29: Ch3, dc2tog, 10 (13)dc, 2hdc, 4sc - 18 (21) sts. Fasten off.

Sizes L and XL only

Row 24: Ch1, 7sc, [1Cl, 5sc] 3 times, 1Cl, 6sc, turn.
Row 25: Dc2tog, dc to end, turn - 31 sts.
Row 26: Ch1, 4sc, 1cl, [5sc, 1Cl] 4 times, 2sc, turn
Row 27: Dc2tog, dc to last 5 sts, 1hdc, 4sc, turn, fasten off - 30 sts.
Row 28: Miss 4sc and 1hdc and rejoin yarn in top of next st, 8sc, [1Cl, 5sc] twice, 1Cl, 4sc turn - 25 sts
Row 29: Ch3, dc2tog, 16dc, 2hdc, 4sc - 24 sts Fasten off.

BACK (all sizes)

Work as for Front to **.
Rows 22-26: Work in pattern as set.
Row 27: Ch1, 4sc, 1hdc, dc to last 5 sts, 1hdc, 4sc, fasten off.
Row 28: Rejoin yarn in top of first hdc, 1ch, patt to last 14 sts, 8sc, turn.
Row 29: Ch1, 4sc, 2hdc, dc to last 6 sts, 2hdc, 4sc. Fasten off.

SLEEVES (both alike)

CUFFS

Work 28 (28, 32, 32) rows in rib as for Front Welt using USJ-9/5.5mm hook

Change to USJ-10/6mm hook evenly distribute 28 (28, 32, 32)sc along long edge of cuff, turn.

Row 1: Ch3 (counts as 1dc here and throughout), 1sc, [1dc, 1sc] to end, turn – 28 (28, 32, 32) sts.
Row 2 (inc): Ch3, [1sc, 1dc] to last st, (1sc, 1dc) in last st, turn - 29 (29, 33, 33) sts.
Row 3 (inc): Ch1 (does not count as st here and throughout), 1sc in first dc, 1dc, [1sc, 1dc] to last st, (1sc, 1dc) in last st, turn - 30 (30, 34, 34) sts.
Row 4 (inc): Ch1, 1sc in first dc, [1dc, 1sc] to last st, (1dc, 1sc) in last sc, turn - 31 (31, 35, 35) sts.
Row 5 (inc): Ch3, 1sc in first dc, [1dc, 1sc] to last sc, (1dc, 1sc) in last sc, turn - 32 (32, 36, 36) sts.
Row 6 (inc): Ch3, 1sc in first dc, 1dc, [1sc, 1dc] to last st, (1sc, 1dc) in last st, turn - 33 (33, 37, 37) sts.
Row 7: Ch1, 1sc in first dc, [1dc, 1sc] to end, turn.
Row 8: Ch3, 1sc in first dc, 1dc, [1sc, 1dc] to end, turn.
Row 9: Ch1, 1sc in first dc, [1dc, 1sc] to end, turn.
Row 10: Ch3, 1sc in first dc, 1dc, [1sc, 1dc] to end, turn.
Row 11: Ch1, 1sc in first dc, [1dc, 1sc] to end, turn.
Row 12: Rep row 10.
Row 13: Rep row 11.
Row 14 (inc): Rep row 5 - 34 (34, 38, 38) sts.
Row 15 (inc): Rep row 6 - 35 (35, 39, 39) sts.
Row 16 (inc): Rep row 3 - 36 (36, 40, 40) sts.
Row 17 (inc): Rep row 4 - 37 (37, 41, 41) sts.
Row 18 (inc): Rep row 5 - 38 (38, 42, 42) sts.

Row 19 (inc): Rep row 6 - 39 (39, 43, 43) sts.
Row 20: Rep row 7.
Row 21: Rep row 8.
Row 22: Rep row 9.
Rows 23-30: Rep rows 10 and 11.

Sizes L and XL only

Rows 31-32: Rep rows 10 and 11.

All sizes

Change to USJ-9/5.5mm hook
Rows 31 (31, 33, 33) - 41 (41, 43, 43): Ch3, 1dc in each st to end.
Fasten off.

TO FINISH

Join at shoulders. Sew in sleeves. Join under arm and sleeve seam.
Join yarn at nape of neck and evenly distribute approx 48 (48, 48, 60)sc around neck edge.
Work 3 rows in sc around.
Fasten off.
Sew in ends.

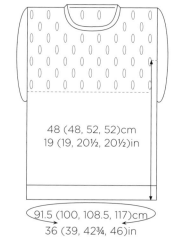

48 (48, 52, 52)cm
19 (19, 20½, 20½)in

91.5 (100, 108.5, 117)cm
36 (39, 42¾, 46)in

Lower Body Pattern

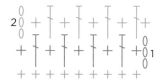

Upper Body Pattern

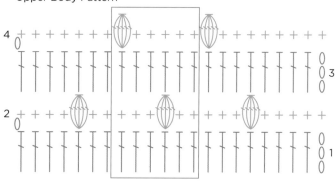

┬ **dc -** double crochet

⬭ **ch -** chain

+ **sc -** single crochet

🔶 **cluster**

▢ Pattern repeat

Going Round in
CIRCLES KIMONO

This cotton Kimono is an absolutely versatile garment - cool enough to wear as a cover up on the beach, a perfect warm up for a summer outfit, or great with your favorite pair of jeans for a casual look!

DIFFICULTY

★ ★ ★ ★

MATERIALS

Scheepjes Bloom, 100% cotton, 50g/80m/87yds
Chrysanthemum 410 x 22 (24, 26, 28) balls
4.5mm/US7 and 5mm/US8 crochet hooks

YARN ALTERNATIVES

You can use any Aran/chunky weight yarn that works to the same tension.

TENSION

Motifs, when blocked, measure:

Small motif – 20cm/8in square
Medium motif – 23cm/9in square
Large motif – 26cm/10¼in square
Extra large motif – 29cm/11½in square

Work 17 sts and 8 rows over double crochet to measure 10 x 10cm/4 x 4in using 4.5mm/US7 hook
Work 16 sts and 8 rows over double crochet to measure 10 x 10cm/4 x 4in using 5mm/US8 hook

PATTERN NOTES

It is essential to block all motifs before joining. The finished garment must also be blocked.

SPECIAL STITCHES

Puff: (yrh, insert hook, yrh, pull up a loop to height of a dc) three times, (7 loops on hook), yrh, pull through all 7 loops, ch1 to close.

Beginning Puff (BegPuff): ch3, *yrh, insert hook, yrh, pull through loop to the height of a dc stitch; rep from * once more (5 loops on hook), yrh pull through all 5 loops, ch1 to close.

MEASUREMENTS

SIZE	S	M	L	XL
Actual bust approx				
	102	111	120	129 cm
	40	43¾	47¾	51 in
Length to shoulder approx				
	69	72	77.5	80 cm
	27	28¼	30½	31¾ in
Sleeve seam approx				
	28	28	28	28 cm
	11	11	11	11 in

PATTERN STARTS

MOTIF (Make 5)

Block all motifs before joining. Fasten off after each row, do not turn work until instructed.
Using 5mm/US8 hook, ch6, sl st to form ring.

Rnd 1: Ch4 counts as (1dc, ch1), [1dc, ch1] 11 times in ring, sl st to 3rd of ch 4. Fasten off.

Rnd 2: Join yarn in any ch1-sp, BegPuff in first ch-sp, ch2, (1Puff, ch2) in each ch-sp, join with sl st. Fasten off.

Rnd 3: Join yarn in any ch2-sp, (BegPuff, ch1, 1Puff, ch1) in first ch2-sp, (1Puff, ch1) in next ch2-sp, *(1Puff, ch1) twice in next ch2-sp, (1Puff, ch1) in next ch2-sp; rep from * around. Fasten off.

Rnd 4: Join yarn in any ch-sp, BegPuff in first ch-sp, ch2, (1Puff, ch2) in each ch-sp, sl st to join. Fasten off.

Rnd 5: Join yarn in ch1-sp, (BegPuff, ch2, 1Puff, ch1) in first ch-sp, (1Puff, ch2, 1Puff, ch1) in each ch2-sp around, sl st to join. Fasten off.

Rnd 6: Join yarn in any ch-sp, (BegPuff, ch1) in next ch-sp, (1Puff, ch1) in each ch1-sp and ch2-sp around, sl st to join. Fasten off. TURN.

Turn after every row from this point:

Rnd 7: Join yarn in any ch-sp, (ch4, 1tr, ch2, 2tr) (first corner made), *3dc in next ch-sp, 3hdc in next ch-sp, 3sc in each of next four ch-sps, 3hdc in next ch-sp, 3dc in next ch-sp, (2tr, ch2, 2tr) in next dc; rep from * twice, 3dc in next ch-sp, 3hdc in each ch-sp, 3sc in each of next four ch-sps, 3hdc in next ch-sp, 3dc in next ch-sp, sl st to join. Fasten off. TURN.

Rnd 8: Join yarn in any corner ch-sp (ch3, 2dc, ch2, 3dc) in corner ch-sp, *3dc in each gap between next 9 groups of 3 sts, (3dc, ch2, 3dc) in corner ch2-sp; rep from * twice more, 3dc in gap between next 9 groups of 3 sts, sl st to join. Fasten off. (Size S finish here).

Rnd 9: Join yarn in any corner ch-sp (ch3, 2dc, ch2, 3dc) in corner ch-sp, *3dc in gap between next 10 groups of 3 sts, (3dc, ch2, 3dc) in corner ch2-sp; rep from * twice more, 3dc in gap between next 10 groups of 3 sts, sl st to join. Fasten off. (Size M finish here).

Rnd 10: Join yarn in any corner ch-sp, (ch3, 2dc, ch2, 3dc) in corner ch-sp, *3dc in gap between next 11 groups of 3 sts, (3dc, ch2, 3dc) in corner ch2-sp; rep from * twice more, 3dc in gap between next 11 groups of 3 sts, sl st to join. Fasten off. (Size L finish here).

Rnd 11: Join yarn in any corner ch-sp (ch3, 2dc, ch2, 3dc) in corner ch-sp, *3dc in gap between next 12 groups of 3 sts (3dc, ch2, 3dc) in corner ch2-sp; rep from * twice more, 3dc in gap between next 12 groups of 3 sts, sl st to join. Fasten off. (Size XL finish here).

JOINING

Block squares.
Sew squares together in a row.

BODY

Using 5mm/US8 hook, working along long edge of motifs, evenly distribute 167 (182, 197, 212) sc.
Rows 1-20: Ch3 (counts as first 1 dc here and throughout), 1dc in each dc to end, turn. Do not break yarn.

RIGHT FRONT

Change to 4.5mm/US7 hook.
Rows 21-34: Ch3, 39 (41, 44, 48)dc, turn - 40 (42, 45, 49)dc.

Sizes L and XL only
Rows 35-36: Rep last row.

All sizes
Fasten off.

BACK

With RS facing and 4.5mm/US7 hook, skip 3 (3, 3, 4) dc and rejoin yarn to next st on row 21.
Row 21: Ch3, 82 (91, 100, 109)dc, turn - 83 (92, 101, 110) dc.
Rows 22-34: Rep last row.

Sizes L and XL only
Rows 35-36: Rep last row.
All sizes
Fasten off.

LEFT FRONT

With RS facing and 4.5mm/US7 hook, skip next 3 dc and rejoin yarn to next st on row 21.
Row 21: Ch3, 39 (41, 44, 48)dc, turn - 40 (42, 45, 49)dc.
Rows 22-34: Rep last row.

Sizes L and XL only
Rows 35-36: Rep last row.

All sizes
Fasten off.

Join shoulder seams. Measure 18 (18, 20, 20)cm down from shoulder and join sides from this point down to bottom edge.

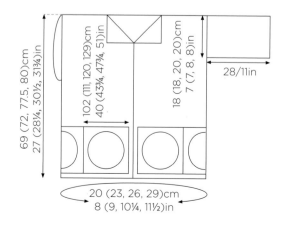

69 (72, 77.5, 80)cm
27 (28¼, 30½, 31¾)in

102 (111, 120, 129)cm
40 (43¾, 47¾, 51)in

18 (18, 20, 20)cm
7 (7, 8, 8)in

28/11in

20 (23, 26, 29)cm
8 (9, 10¼, 11½)in

SLEEVES

With 4.5mm/US7 hook, join yarn at under arm seam, evenly distribute 58 (58, 62, 62)dc around armhole, sl st to join. TURN.

Rows 2-20: Ch3 (counts as 1 dc), dc to end, sl st to join. TURN.

Row 21: Ch1, 1sc in each dc. TURN.

Row 22: Ch1, sc to end.
Fasten off.

FINISHING

Work 2 rows of sc around entire edge of garment.
Block garment.
Sew in ends.

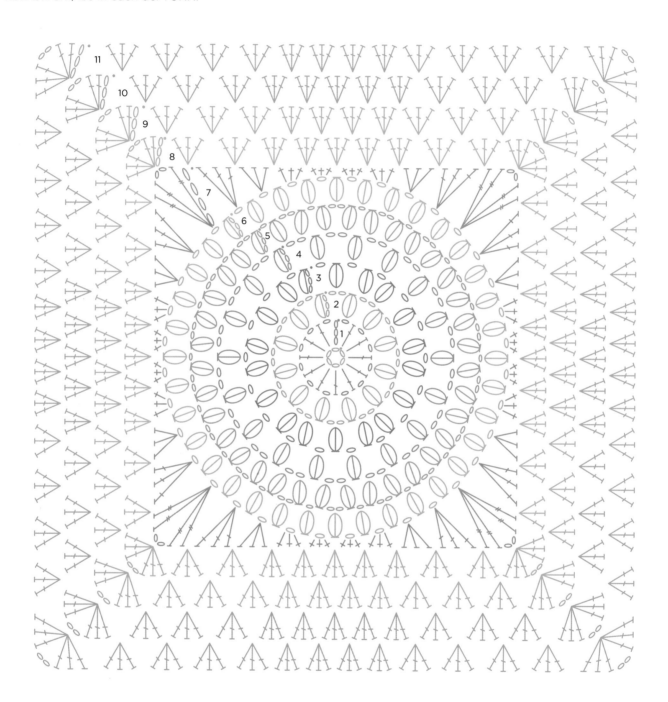

ch - chain	**hdc -** half double crochet	puff	> **Small:** End after round 8.
sc - single crochet			> **Medium:** End after round 9.
sl st - slip stitch	**tr -** treble	beg puff	> **Large:** End after round 10.
dc - double crochet			> **Extra Large:** End after round 11.

Star
CARDIGAN

A beautiful modern pattern, this cardigan is a great wear to take off the winter chill. Its simple yet beautiful pattern is wonderful for every day wear, and is a really fun way to use the bobble texture.

MATERIALS

Scheepjes Whirligigette 80% virgin wool, 20% alpaca, 100g/215m/235yds
Ochre 254 x 9 (9, 12, 12) balls
5mm/US8 and 5.5mm/US9 hooks

YARN ALTERNATIVES

You can use any Dk yarn that works to the same tension.

TENSION

17 sts x 20 rows in single crochet to measure 10 x 10cm/4 x 4in using 5.5mm/US9 hook or size required to obtain tension.

SPECIAL STITCHES

Cluster (Cl): (Yrh, insert hook, yrh draw loop through, yrh, draw through 2 loops) 5 times in next st, yrh draw through all loops on hook.

NB: Clusters are worked on WS rows.

Sc blo: single crochet worked in back loop only

MEASUREMENTS

SIZE	S	M	L	XL
Actual measurement				
	98	107	117	123 cm
	38½	42	46	48½ in
Length				
	61	61	61	61 cm
	24	24	24	24 in
Sleeve length				
	41	42	43	44 cm
	16	16½	17	17½ in

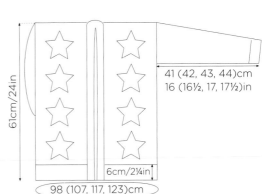

41 (42, 43, 44)cm
16 (16½, 17, 17½)in

61cm/24in

6cm/2¼in

98 (107, 117, 123)cm
38½ (42, 46, 48½)in

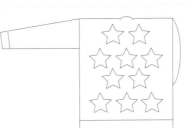

PATTERN STARTS

BACK

WELT

Using 5mm/US8 hook, ch14.

Row 1: 1sc in 2nd ch from hook and in each ch to end, turn - 13sc.

Rows 2-83 (91, 99, 107): Ch1, sc blo to end, turn.
Fasten off.

Using 5.5mm/US9 hook evenly distribute 83 (91, 99, 107) sc along long edge of ribbed welt.

Row 2-6: Ch1 (does not count as st here and throughout), 1sc in each sc to end, turn.

Row 7 (WS): Ch1, 5 (7, 9, 11)sc, *1cl, 1sc, 1cl, 11sc, 1cl, 1sc, 1cl, 11 (13, 15, 17)sc; rep from *, 1cl, 1sc, 1cl, 11sc, 1cl, 1sc, 1cl, 5 (7, 9, 11)sc, turn.

Row 8 and all following RS rows: Ch1, 1sc in each sc and top of each cl to end, turn.

Row 9: Ch1, 5 (7, 9, 11)sc, *1cl, 3sc, 1cl, 7sc, 1cl, 3sc, 1cl, 11 (13, 15, 17)sc; rep from *, 1cl, 3sc, 1cl, 7sc, 1cl, 3sc, 1cl, 5 (7, 9, 11)sc, turn.

Row 11: Ch1, 6 (8, 10, 12)sc, *1cl, 4sc, 1cl, 3sc, 1cl, 4sc, 1cl, 13 (15, 17, 19) sc; rep from *, 1cl, 4sc, 1cl, 3sc, 1cl, 4sc, 1cl, 6 (8, 10, 12)sc, turn.

Row 13: Ch1, 7 (9, 11, 13)sc, *[1cl, 5sc] twice, 1cl, 15 (17, 19, 21)sc; rep from *, [1cl, 5sc] twice, 1cl, 7 (9, 11, 13) sc, turn.

Row 15: Ch1, 8 (10, 12, 14)sc, *1cl, 9sc, 1cl, 17 (19, 21, 23)sc; rep from *, 1cl, 9sc, 1cl, 8 (10, 12, 14)sc, turn.

Row 17: Ch1, 6 (8, 10, 12)sc, *1cl, 13sc, 1cl, 13 (15, 17, 19)sc; rep from *, 1cl, 13sc, 1cl, 6 (8, 10, 12)sc, turn.

Row 19: Ch1, 4 (6, 8, 10)sc, 1cl, 17sc, 1cl, 9 (11, 13, 15)sc; rep from *, 1cl, 17sc, 1cl, 4 (6, 8, 10)sc, turn.

Row 21: Ch1, 3 (5, 7, 9)sc, *[1cl, 1sc] three times, 1cl, 7sc, [1cl, 1sc] three times, 1cl, 7 (9, 11, 13)sc; rep from *, [1cl, 1sc] three times, 1cl, 7sc, [1cl, 1sc] three times, 1cl, 3 (5, 7, 9)sc, turn.

Row 23: Ch1, 10 (12, 14, 16)sc, *1cl, 5sc, 1cl, 21 (23, 25, 27) sc; rep from *, 1cl, 5sc, 1cl, 10 (12, 14, 16)sc, turn.

Row 25: Ch1, 11 (13, 15, 17)sc, *1cl, 3sc, 1cl, 23 (25, 27, 29)sc; rep from *, 1cl, 3sc, 1cl, 11 (13, 15, 17)sc, turn.

Row 27: Ch1, 12 (14, 16, 18)sc, *1cl, 1sc, 1cl, 25 (27, 29, 31)sc; rep from *, 1cl, 1sc, 1cl, 12 (14, 16, 18)sc, turn.

Row 29: Ch1, 13 (15, 17, 19)sc, *1cl, 27 (29, 31, 33)sc; rep from *, 1cl, 13 (15, 17, 19)sc, turn.

Rows 30-32: Rep row 8.

Row 33: Ch1, 19 (22, 25, 28)sc, 1cl, 1sc, 1cl, 11sc, 1cl, 1sc, 1cl, 11 (13, 15, 17)sc, 1cl, 1sc, 1cl, 11sc, 1cl, 1sc, 1cl, 19 (22, 25, 28) sc, turn.

Row 35: Ch1, 19 (22, 25, 28)sc, 1cl, 3sc, 1cl, 7sc, 1cl, 3sc, 1cl, 11 (13, 15, 17)sc, 1cl, 3sc, 1cl, 7sc, 1cl, 3sc, 1cl, 19 (22, 25, 28) sc, turn.

Row 37: Ch1, 20 (23, 26, 29)sc, 1cl, 4sc, 1cl, 3sc, 1cl, 4sc, 1cl, 13 (15, 17, 19)sc, 1cl, 4sc, 1cl, 3sc, 1cl, 4sc, 1cl, 20 (23, 26, 29)sc, turn.

Row 39: Ch1, 21 (24, 27, 30)sc, [1cl, 5sc] twice, 1cl, 15 (17, 19, 21)sc, [1cl, 5sc] twice, 1cl, 21 (24, 27, 30)sc, turn.

Row 41: Ch1, 22 (25, 28, 31)sc, 1cl, 9sc, 1cl, 17 (19, 21, 23)sc, 1cl, 9sc, 1cl, 22 (25, 28, 31)sc.

Row 43: Ch1, 20 (23, 26, 29)sc, 1cl, 13sc, 1cl, 13 (15, 17, 19) sc, 1cl, 13sc, 1cl, 20 (23, 26, 29)sc, turn.

Row 45: Ch1, 18 (21, 24, 27)sc, 1cl, 17sc, 1cl, 9 (11, 13, 15)sc, 1cl, 17sc, 1cl, 18 (21, 24, 27)sc, turn.

Row 47: Ch1, 17 (20, 23, 26)sc, [1cl, 1sc] three times, 1cl, 7sc, [1cl, 1sc] three times, 1cl, 7 (9, 11, 13)sc, [1cl, 1sc] three times, 1cl, 7sc, [1cl, 1sc] three times, 1cl, 17 (20, 23, 26)sc, turn.

Row 49: Ch1, 24 (27, 30, 33)sc, 1cl, 5sc, 1cl, 21 (23, 25, 27) sc, 1cl, 5sc, 1cl, 24 (27, 30, 33)sc, turn.

Row 51: Ch1, 25 (28, 31, 34)sc, 1cl, 3sc, 1cl, 23 (25, 27, 29) sc, 1cl, 3sc, 1cl, 25 (28, 31, 34)sc, turn.

Row 53: Ch1, 26 (29, 32, 35)sc, 1cl, 1sc, 1cl, 25 (27, 29, 31) sc, 1cl, 1sc, 1cl, 26 (29, 32, 35)sc, turn.

Row 55: Ch1, 27 (30, 33, 36)sc, 1cl, 27 (29, 31, 33)sc, 1cl, 27 (30, 33, 36)sc, turn.

Rows 56-58: Ch1, 1sc in each st to end, turn.
Repeat rows 7-58 once more.

Final row: 13 (15, 17, 19) sl st, 57 (61, 65, 69)sc, 13 (15, 17, 19) sl st.
Fasten off.

RIGHT FRONT

WELT

Using 5mm/US8 hook, ch14.

Row 1: 1sc in 2nd ch from hook and in each ch to end, turn - 13sc.

Rows 2-37 (41, 45, 49): Ch1, sc blo to end, turn.
Fasten off.

Using 5.5mm/US9 hook, evenly distribute 37 (41, 45, 49) sc along long edge of ribbed welt.

Rows 2-6: Ch1 (does not count as st here and throughout), 1sc in each sc to end, turn.

Row 7 (WS): Ch1, 10 (12, 14, 16)sc, 1cl, 1sc, 1cl, 11sc, 1cl, 1sc, 1cl, 10 (12, 14, 16)sc, turn.

Row 8 and all foll RS rows: Ch1, 1sc in each sc and top of each cl to end, turn.

Row 9: Ch1, 10 (12, 14, 16)sc, 1cl, 3sc, 1cl, 7sc, 1cl, 3sc, 1cl, 10 (12, 14, 16)sc, turn.

Row 11: Ch1, 11 (13, 15, 17)sc, 1cl, 4sc, 1cl, 3sc, 1cl, 4sc, 1cl, 11 (13, 15, 17)sc, turn.

Row 13: Ch1, 12 (14, 16, 18)sc, [1cl, 5sc] twice, 1cl, 12 (14, 16, 18)sc, turn.

Row 15: Ch1, 13 (15, 17, 19)sc, 1cl, 9sc, 1cl, 13 (15, 17, 19)sc, turn.

Row 17: Ch1, 11 (13, 15, 17)sc, 1cl, 13sc, 1cl, 11 (13, 15, 17)sc, turn.

Row 19: Ch1, 9 (11, 13, 15)sc, 1cl, 17sc, 1cl, 9 (11, 13, 15)sc, turn.

Thé

colat

nade

acao

Row 21: Ch1, 8 (10, 12, 14)sc, [1cl, 1sc] three times, 1cl, 7sc, 1cl, [1sc, 1cl] three times, 8 (10, 12, 14)sc, turn.
Row 23: Ch1, 15 (17, 19, 21)sc, 1cl, 5sc, 1cl, 15 (17, 19, 21)sc, turn.
Row 25: Ch1, 16 (18, 20, 22)sc, 1cl, 3sc, 1cl, 16 (18, 20, 22) sc, turn.
Row 27: Ch1, 17 (19, 21, 23)sc, 1cl, 1sc, 1cl, 17 (19, 21, 23)sc, turn.
Row 29: Ch1, 18 (20, 22, 24)sc, 1cl, 18 (20, 22, 24)sc, turn.
Rows 30-32: Rep row 8.
Rep rows 7 to 32 a further three times.**
Final row: 13 (15, 17, 19) sl st, 24 (26, 28, 30)sc.
Fasten off.

LEFT FRONT

Work as for Right Front to **.
Final row: Ch1, 24 (26, 28, 30)sc, 13 (15, 17, 19) sl st.
Fasten off.

SLEEVES (both alike)

CUFF

Using 5mm/US8 hook, ch14.
Row 1: 1sc in 2nd ch from hook and in each ch to end, turn - 13sc.
Rows 2 - 32 (36, 38, 40): Ch1, sc blo to end, turn.
Fasten off.
Using 5.5mm/US9 hook evenly distribute 32 (36, 38, 40) sc along long edge of ribbed welt.
Row 1: Ch1 (does not count as st here and throughout), 31 (35, 37, 39)sc, 2sc in last sc, turn - 33 (37, 39, 41)sc.
Row 2: Ch1, 32 (36, 38, 40)sc, 2sc in last sc, turn - 34 (38, 40, 42)sc.
Rows 3-4: Ch1, 1sc in each sc to end, turn.
Rows 5-8: Rep rows 1-4 once more - 36 (40, 42, 44)sc.
Rows 9-14: Ch1, 1sc in each sc to end, turn.
Rows 15-16: Rep rows 1-2 - 38 (42, 44, 46)sc.
Row 17-22: Ch1, 1sc in each sc to end, turn.
Rep rows 15-22 a further six times.

Star Chart

Cluster   Single Crochet

Size S only
Fasten off.

Sizes M, L and XL only
Row 71: Ch1, 1sc in each sc to end, turn.
Rep last row 1 (3, 5) more times.
Fasten off.

TO MAKE UP

Join at shoulders. Sew in sleeves. Join under arm and sleeve seam.

FRONT EDGING

With RS facing, using 5mm/US8 hook, evenly distribute 254sc around fronts and neck, turn.
Row 1: Ch2 (counts as 1dc here and throughout), 1dc in each sc to end, turn.
Row 2: Ch2, [1fpdc, 1bpdc] to last st, 1dc, turn.
Row 3: Ch2, [1bpdc, 1fpdc] to last st, 1dc.
Fasten off.

TO FINISH

Darn in ends.

Loop
STITCH JACKET

This fun loop stitch jacket is playful and on trend. It can be made in any colorway, a real head turner and bang on trend. A simple first garment piece that will leave you the envy of all your friends.

DIFFICULTY

★ ★

MATERIALS

Scheepjes Eliza, 100% polyester, 100g/230m/252yds
Cornflower 216 x 13(14, 16, 18) balls
4.5mm/US7 crochet hook

YARN ALTERNATIVES

You can use any DK weight yarn that works to the same tension.

TENSION

16.5 sts x 18 rows in Loop Stitch to measure 10 x 10cm/4 x 4in using 4.5mm/US7 hook or size required to obtain tension.

SPECIAL STITCHES

Loop stitch = working from WS, wrap yarn back to front around and over the index finger holding the yarn, (pull out a loop approx 4cm/1½in long). Insert hook in next stitch, grab the yarn from behind your index finger and draw the yarn through the stitch. With the loop still on your finger, yrh hook and draw through both loops on hook. Repeat in each stitch across.

Try to ensure all loops are equal size.

MEASUREMENTS

SIZE	S	M	L	XL
Actual bust approx				
	97	109	121	133 cm
	38	43	47½	52¼ in
Back width at bottom edge				
	54.5	60	66.5	73 cm
	21½	23¾	26¼	28¾ in
Length approx				
	61	61	64.5	64.5 cm
	24	24	25½	25½ in
Sleeve length				
	47	47	47	47 cm
	18½	18½	18½	18½ in

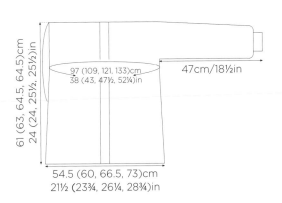

61 (63, 64.5, 64.5)cm
24 (24, 25½, 25½)in

97 (109, 121, 133)cm
38 (43, 47½, 52¼)in

47cm/18½in

54.5 (60, 66.5, 73)cm
21½ (23¾, 26¼, 28¾)in

BACK

Using 4.5mm/US7 hook, 91 (101, 111, 121)ch.

Row 1: 1sc in 2nd ch from hook and in each ch to end, turn - 90 (100, 110, 120)sc.

Row 2: Ch1 (does not count as st here and throughout), 1lp st in each sc to end, turn.

Row 3: Ch1, 1sc in each st to end, turn.

Row 4-6: Rep rows 2 and 3 ending on row 2.

Row 7: Sc2tog, 1sc in each st to last 2 sts, sc2tog, turn - 88 (98, 108, 118)sc.

Row 8-22: Rep rows 2 and 3 ending on row 2.

Row 23: Rep row 7 - 86 (96, 106, 116)sc.

Row 24-46: Rep rows 2 and 3 ending on row 2

Row 47: Rep row 7 - 84 (94, 104, 114)sc.

Rows 48-56: Rep rows 2 and 3 ending on row 2.

Row 57: Rep row 7 - 82 (92, 102, 112)sc.

Rows 58-68: Rep rows 2 and 3 ending on row 2.

Row 69: Rep row 7 - 80 (90, 100, 110)sc.

Rows 70-88: Rep rows 2 and 3 ending on row 2.

Row 89: Rep row 7 - 78 (88, 98, 108)sc.

Rows 90-110 (110, 116, 116): Rep rows 2 and 3 ending on row 2.

Fasten off.

LEFT FRONT

Using 4.5mm/US7 hook, 41 (46, 51, 56)ch.

Row 1: 1sc in 2nd ch from hook and in each ch to end, turn - 40 (45, 50, 55)sc.

Row 2: Ch1 (does not count as st here and throughout), 1lp st in each sc to end, turn.

Row 3: Ch1, 1sc in each st to end, turn.

Row 4-6: Rep rows 2 and 3 ending on row 2.

Row 7: Sc2tog, 1sc in each st to end, turn - 39 (44, 49, 54)sc.

Row 8-22: Rep rows 2 and 3 ending on row 2.

Row 23: Rep row 7 - 38 (43, 48, 53)sc.

Row 24-46: Rep rows 2 and 3 ending on row 2

Row 47: Rep row 7 - 37 (42, 47, 52)sc.

Rows 48-56: Rep rows 2 and 3 ending on row 2.

Row 57: Rep row 7 - 36 (41, 46, 51)sc.

Rows 58-68: Rep rows 2 and 3 ending on row 2.

Row 69: Rep row 7 - 35 (40, 45, 50)sc.

Rows 70-88: Rep rows 2 and 3 ending on row 2.

Row 89: Rep row 7 - 34 (39, 44, 49)sc.

Rows 90-110 (110, 116, 116): Rep rows 2 and 3 ending on row 2.

Fasten off.

RIGHT FRONT

Using 4.5mm/US7 hook, 41 (46, 51, 56)ch.

Row 1: 1sc in 2nd ch from hook and in each ch to end, turn - 40 (45, 50, 55)sc.

Row 2: Ch1 (does not count as st here and throughout), 1lp st in each sc to end turn.

Row 3: Ch1, 1sc in each st to end, turn.

Row 4-6: Rep rows 2 and 3 ending on row 2.

Row 7: Ch1 (does not count as st), 1sc in each st to last 2 sts, sc2tog, turn - 39 (44, 49, 54)sc.

Row 8-22: Rep rows 2 and 3 ending on row 2.

Row 23: Rep row 7 - 38 (43, 48, 53)sc.

Row 24-46: Rep rows 2 and 3 ending on row 2

Row 47: Rep row 7 - 37 (42, 47, 52)sc.

Rows 48-56: Rep rows 2 and 3 ending on row 2.

Row 57: Rep row 7 - 36 (41, 46, 51)sc.

Rows 58-68: Rep rows 2 and 3 ending on row 2.

Row 69: Rep row 7 - 35 (40, 45, 50)sc.

Rows 70-88: Rep rows 2 and 3 ending on row 2.

Row 89: Rep row 7 - 34 (39, 44, 49)sc.

Rows 90-110 (110, 116, 116): Rep rows 2 and 3 ending on row 2.

Fasten off.

SLEEVES (both alike)

Cuffs

With 4.5mm/US7 hook, ch8.

Row 1: 1sc in 2nd ch from hook and in each ch to end, turn - 7sc.

Rows 2-25 (25, 29, 29): Ch1 (does not count as st here and throughout), 1sc blo of each st to end, turn, working along long edge of cuff as folls:

Row 1: Evenly distribute 25 (25, 29, 29)sc, turn.

Row 2: Ch1, 2lp sts in each st to end, turn - 50 (50, 58, 58) sts.

Row 3: Ch1, 1sc in each st to end, turn.

Row 4: Ch1, 1lp st in each st to end, turn.

Rows 5-72: Rep rows 3 and 4.

Fasten off.

POCKETS (all sizes)

Using 4.5mm/US7 hook, ch31.

Row 1: 1sc in 2nd ch from hook and in each ch to end, turn - 30sc.

Row 2: Ch1, 1lp st in each st to end, turn.

Row 3: Ch1, 1sc in each st to end, turn.

Rows 4-27: Rep rows 2 and 3.

Row 28: Ch1, 1sc in each st to end, turn.

Fasten off.

TO FINISH

Sew Front to Back along shoulders. Measure down approx 16 (16, 18, 18)cm/6 (6, 7, 7)in from shoulder seam and place marker on each side. Sew Sleeve head between markers. Sew side and sleeve seams.

Using 4.5mm/US7 hook, work 2 rows in sc around neck edge.

Sew on pockets.

Darn in ends.

Balloon Stitch
MAXI CARDIGAN

This super soft, feel good knee length cardigan is like a warm soft hug. Not only is it bang on trend but it gives your spirit an instant lift every time you slip it on. Relax in a pair of your favorite jeans or make that outfit just a little more cosy with this delightful statement piece.

DIFFICULTY

★ ★ ★ ★

MATERIALS

Scheepjes Stone Washed XL 70% cotton, 30% acrylic, 50g/75m/82yds
Moon Stone 841 x 34 (36, 38, 40) 50g balls
Size S: 5.5mm/US9/I and 6mm/US10/J hooks
Size M: 6.5mm/US10½/K and 7mm hooks
Size L: 7.5mm and 8mm/US11/L hooks
Size XL: 8.5mm and 9mm/US13 hooks

YARN ALTERNATIVES

You can use any Aran weight yarn that works to the same tension.

TENSION

Work 18 (16, 14, 12) sts x 11 (10, 9, 8) rows in patt to measure 10 x 10cm/4 x 4in using 6mm/US10/J (7mm, 8mm/US11/L, 9mm/US13) hook or size required to obtain tension.

MEASUREMENTS

SIZE	S	M	L	XL
Actual bust approx				
	94	107	122	145 cm
	37	42	48	57 in
Length to shoulder approx				
	72	80	78	83 cm
	28½	31½	30¾	32¾ in
Sleeve seam approx				
	47	52	50	51 cm
	18	20½	19¾	20 in

BACK

Using 6mm/US10/J (7mm, 8mm/US11/L, 9mm/US13) hook, ch89.

Work in Balloon Stitch as folls:

Row 1: (Foundation row) 4dc in 4th ch from hook, 1dc in each of next 2 ch, dc7tog over next 7 ch, *1dc in each of next 2 ch, 7dc in next ch, 1dc in each of next 2 ch, dc7tog over next 7 ch; rep from * to last 4 ch, 1dc in each of next 2 ch, 4dc in next ch, 1dc in last ch, turn.

Row 2: Ch3 (counts as 1dc here and throughout), 4fpdc, 2bpdc, 1fpdc in top of dc7tog, *2bpdc, 7fpdc, 2bpdc, 1fpdc (in top of dc7tog); rep from * to last 7 sts, 2bpdc, 4fpdc, 1dc in top of ch 3, turn.

Row 3: Ch3, 4bpdc, 2fpdc, 1bpdc, [2fpdc, 7bpdc, 2fpdc, 1bpdc] to last 7 sts, 2fpdc, 4bpdc, 1dc in top of ch 3, turn.

Row 4: Ch3, 4fpdc, 2bpdc, 1fpdc, [2bpdc, 7fpdc, 2bpdc, 1fpdc] to last 7 sts, 2bpdc, 4fpdc, 1dc in top of ch 3, turn.

Row 5: Ch3, bpdc4tog, 2fpdc, [7dc in top of next 1bpdc, 2fpdc, bpdc7tog, 2fpdc] to last 8 sts, 7dc in top of next 1bpdc, 2fpdc, bpdc4tog, 1dc in top of ch 3, turn.

Row 6: Ch3, 1fpdc in top of bpdc4tog, 2bpdc, 7fpdc, 2bpdc, [1fpdc in top of bpdc7tog, 2bpdc, 7fpdc, 2bpdc] to last 2 sts, 1fpdc in top of bpdc4tog, 1dc in top of ch 3, turn.

Row 7: Ch3, 1bpdc, [2fpdc, 7bpdc, 2fpdc, 1bpdc] to last st, 1dc in top of ch3, turn.

Row 8: Ch3, 1fpdc, [2bpdc, 7fpdc, 2bpdc, 1fpdc] to end, 1dc in top of last ch 3, turn.

Row 9: Ch3, 4dc in top of 1fpdc of last row, 2fpdc, bpdc-7tog, 2fpdc, [7dc in top of fpdc, 2fpdc, bpdc7tog, 2fpdc,] to last 2 sts, 4dc in top of last fpdc, 1dc in top of ch 3, turn.

Rows 2-9 form pattern and are repeated.
Rep rows 2-9 a further 7 (7, 6, 6) times.
Rep rows 2-3.
Fasten off.

FRONT (make two alike)

Using 6mm/US10/J (7mm, 8mm/US11/L, 9mm/US13) hook ch41.
Work in patt as for Back.

SLEEVES

Using 6mm/US10/J (7mm, 8mm/US11/L, 9mm/US13) hook, 53ch.
Beg from row 1, work in Balloon Stitch as for Back for a total of 38 (38, 33, 30) rows ending on patt row 6 (6, 9, 6).
Finishing rows 1-3: Ch1, 1sc in each st, turn.
Fasten off.

CUFF (make two)

Sew along length of arm (sc rows are top edge of arm).
With 5.5mm/US9/I (6.5mm/US10½/K, 7.5mm, 8.5mm) hook, 15ch.
Row 1: 1sc in 2nd ch from hook, 1sc in each ch to end, turn - 14sc
Rows 2-22: Ch1, sc blo to end, turn.
Fasten off.

BOTTOM RIBBING

With 5.5mm/US9/I (6.5mm/US10½/K, 7.5mm, 8.5mm) hook, 15ch.
Row 1: 1sc in 2nd ch from hook, 1sc in each ch to end, turn - 14sc.
Rows 2-84: Ch1, sc blo to end, turn.
Fasten off.

TO FINISH

Sew front to back along shoulders.
Sew up along sides leaving approx 19 (21, 23, 25)cm, 7½ (8¼,9, 10)in open for armhole.
Sew in sleeves.
Sew in cuffs stretching to fit the slightly larger arm this gives a balloon effect to sleeve.
Sew on bottom ribbing.
Sew in ends.

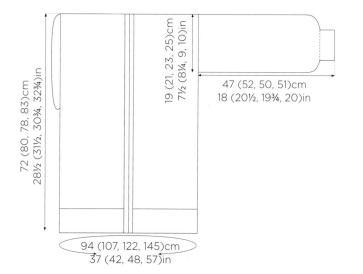

72 (80, 78, 83)cm
28½ (31½, 30¾, 32¾)in

19 (21, 23, 25)cm
7½ (8¼, 9, 10)in

47 (52, 50, 51)cm
18 (20½, 19¾, 20)in

94 (107, 122, 145)cm
37 (42, 48, 57)in

Rep rows 2-9 for pattern

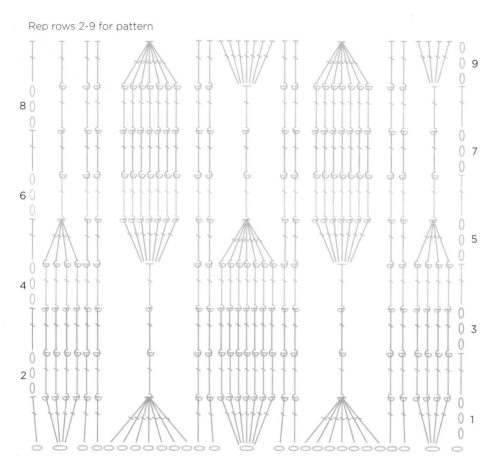

ch - chain

dc - double crochet

fpdc - front post double crochet

bpdc - back post double crochet

bpdc4tog - back post double crochet four together

bpdc7tog - back post double crochet seven together

dc7tog - double crochet seven together

Flower
PONCHO

This beautiful motif based poncho is sure to keep you nice and warm. The pretty pattern makes it a very versatile item.

DIFFICULTY
★ ★ ★ ★

MATERIALS
Scheepjes Merino Soft, 50% Wool Superwash Merino, 25% microfibre, 25% acrylic, 50g/105m/114yds
Da Vinci 606 x 13 (14, 16, 18) balls
3.5mm/US4-E and 4.5mm/US7 crochet hooks

YARN ALTERNATIVES
You can use any DK weight yarn that works to the same tension.

TENSION
Measured from corner to corner, using 4.5mm/US7 hook each Motif measures approx:
Small Motif - 21cm/8¼in
Medium Motif - 23cm/9in
Large Motif - 25cm/9¾in
XL Motif - 27cm/10½in

MEASUREMENTS

SIZE	S	M	L	XL
Width at widest point approx				
	91	100	108	117 cm
	36	39½	42½	46 in
Length approx				
	41	46	50	54 cm
	16	18	19¾	21¼ in

MOTIF (make 18)

With 4.5mm/US7 hook, ch5, sl st to form a ring.

Rnd 1: Ch3 (counts as 1dc here and throughout) 23dc in ring, sl st in top of ch 3 - 24dc.

Rnd 2: [Ch3, skip 1 dc, 1sc in next st] 12 times around, sl st in starting ch3-sp - 12 x ch3-sps.

Rnd 3: Ch3, 3dc in same ch3-sp, ch2, skip next ch3-sp, *4dc in next ch3-sp, ch2, skip next ch3-sp; rep from * 4 more times, sl st in top of ch 3 - 6 x ch2-sps and 24dc.

Rnd 4: Ch3, 1dc in same dc, 2dc, 2dc in next dc, ch2, *(2dc in next dc, 2dc in next dc), ch2; rep from * 4 more times, sl st in top of ch 3 - 6 x ch2-sps, and 36dc.

Rnd 5: Ch3, 1dc in same dc, 4dc, 2dc in next dc, ch2, *(2dc in next dc, 4dc, 2dc in next dc), ch2; rep from * 4 more times, sl st in top of ch 3 - 6 x ch2-sps, and 48dc.

Rnd 6: Ch3, 7dc, (ch3, 1sc, ch3) in ch3-sp, *8dc, (ch3, 1sc, ch3) in ch3-sp; rep from * 4 more times, sl st in top of ch 3 - 12 x ch2-sps, 6sc and 48dc.

Rnd 7: Sl st to 2nd dc of 8 dc group, ch3, 5dc, ch3, 1sc in next ch3-sp, ch3, 1sc in next ch3-sp, ch3, skip 1 dc, *6dc, [ch3, 1sc in next ch3-sp] twice, ch3; rep from * 4 more times, sl st in top of ch 3- 18 x ch3-sps, 12 sc, 36dc.

Rnd 8: Sl st to 2nd dc of 6 dc group, ch3, 3dc, [ch3, 1sc in next ch3-sp] three times, ch3, skip 1 dc, *4dc, [ch3, 1sc in next ch3-sp] three times, ch3; rep from * 4 more times, sl st in top of ch 3, fasten off - 24 x ch3-sps, 18sc, 24dc.

Rnd 9: Sl st across next dc, sl st in space before next dc, ch3, 1dc in same sp, [ch3, 1sc in next ch3-sp] 4 times, ch3, *skip 2 dc, 2dc in space before next dc, [ch3, 1sc in next ch3-sp] 4 times, ch3; rep from 4 more times, sl st in top of ch 3 - 30 x ch3-sps, 24sc, 12dc.

Rnd 10: Sl st between 2 dc, ch3, 1sc in same sp, [ch3, 1sc in next ch3-sp] 5 times, ch3, *(1sc, ch3, 1sc) between 2 dc, [ch3, 1sc, in next ch3-sp] 5 times, ch3; rep from * 4 more times, sl st in first sc - 36 x ch3-sps, 30sc, 6 x (1sc, ch3, 1sc) corners.

Rnd 11: Sl st in corner ch3-sp, ch3 (counts as 1dc), (1dc, ch2, 2dc) in same corner ch3-sp, 2dc in each of next 6 ch3-sps, *(2dc, ch2, 2dc) in corner ch3-sp, 2dc in each of next 6 ch3-sps; rep from * 4 more times, sl st in top of ch 3, fasten off for Size S only - 72 dc, 6 x (2dc, ch2, 2dc) corners.

Sizes M, L and XL only

Rnd 12: Sl st in ch3-sp, (ch3, 1dc, ch2, 2dc) in same corner ch3-sp, 1dc in each st to corner ch3-sp, *(2dc, ch2, 2dc) in corner ch3-sp, 1dc in each st to corner ch3-sp; rep from * 4 more times - 96 dc, 6 x (2dc, ch2, 2dc) corners.

Sizes L and XL only

Rnd 13: Rep rnd 12 - 120 dc, 6 x (2dc, ch2, 2dc) corners.

Size XL only

Rnd 14: Rep rnd 12 -144 dc, 6 x (2dc, ch2, 2dc) corners.

TO MAKE UP

Block all 18 hexagons
Sew hexagons together working in back loop only of every stitch.

NECK EDGING

With 3.5mm/US4-E hook, work 2 rows in sc around neck.
Fasten off.

EDGING

With 4.5mm/US7 hook, work 1 row in sc around bottom edge.
Fasten off.

TO FINISH

Darn in ends.

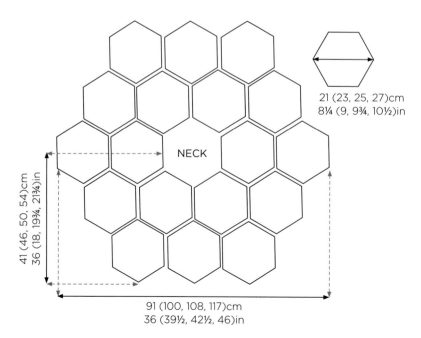

21 (23, 25, 27)cm
8¼ (9, 9¾, 10½)in

NECK

41 (46, 50, 54)cm
36 (18, 19¾, 21¾)in

91 (100, 108, 117)cm
36 (39½, 42½, 46)in

○ **ch -** chain   + **sc -** single crochet   ⊤ **dc -** double crochet   • **sl st -** slip stitch

Ring of
ROSES TOP

This pretty sleeveless jumper has three dimensional roses which give a really pretty and realistic look.

DIFFICULTY

★ ★ ★ ★

MATERIALS

Scheepjes Stone Washed, 78% cotton, 22% acrylic, 50g/130m/142yds
Rose Quartz 820 x 8 (9, 10, 11) balls
3.5mm/US4 and 4mm/US6-G crochet hooks

YARN ALTERNATIVES

You can use any DK yarn that works to the same tension.

TENSION

16 sts and 10 rows in granny stitch pattern to measure 10 x 10cm/4 x 4in using 4mm/US6-G hook, or size required to obtain tension.

Each motif measures 8cm/3¼in square

MEASUREMENTS

SIZE	S	M	L	XL
Actual chest				
	96.5	101	109	113 cm
	38	40	43	44½ in
Length approx				
	46	47	48	49 cm
	18	18½	19	19¼ in

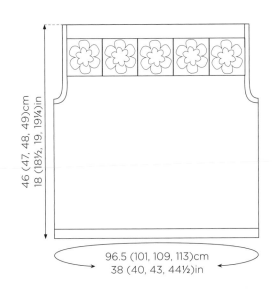

46 (47, 48, 49)cm
18 (18½, 19, 19¼)in

96.5 (101, 109, 113)cm
38 (40, 43, 44½)in

PATTERN STARTS

BACK

(Worked from top down)

With 4mm/US6-G hook, ch62.

Row 1: 1sc in 2nd ch from hook and in each ch to end, turn - 61sc.

Rows 2-5: Ch1 (does not count as st here and throughout), sc to end, turn.

Row 6: Ch3, (counts as 1dc here and throughout), 1dc in same sc, miss 2 sc, *3dc in next sc, miss 2 sc; rep from * to last st, 2dc in last st, turn - 20 x 3dc groups plus 2dc at each end.

Row 7: Ch3, 3dc in space before next 3 dc group, 3dc in each space between 3dc groups to end working last 3dc in space before last 2 sts, 1dc in top of ch 3, turn.

**Row 8: Ch3, 1dc in same st, 3dc in each space between 3dc groups to last st, 2dc in top of ch 3, turn.

Rows 9-14: Rep rows 7 and 8.

Shape armholes

Row 15 (increase): Ch3, 2dc in same st, 3dc in each space between 3 dc groups to last st, 3dc in last dc, turn (3 sts inc'd).

Rows 16-18 (19, 21, 22): As row 15.

Rows 19-46 (20-47, 22-48, 23-49): Work in patt without shaping.

Fasten off. **

FRONT

MOTIF (make 5)

With 4mm/US6-G hook, ch4, sl st to form a ring.

Rnd 1: Ch4, (counts as 1dc, 1ch), (1dc, 1ch) 7 times in ring, sl st to join.

Rnd 2: Sl st to first ch1-sp, (1sc, 2dc, 1sc) in each ch1-sp around - 8 petals

Rnd 3: Working behind petals made on rnd 2, insert hook from back to front to back, work 1sl st behind first dc of rnd 1, *ch3, inserting hook from back to front to back work 1 sc around next dc; rep from * around - 8 ch3-sps

Rnd 4: Sl st in next ch3-sp, work (1sc, 1hdc, 3dc, 1hdc, 1sc) in each ch3-sp around.

Rnd 5: Working behind petals made on rnd 4, inserting hook from back to front to back, sl st behind next sc made on rnd 3, *4ch, 1sc around next sc on rnd 3; rep from * around.

Rnd 6: Rep rnd 4 working into each ch-4sp.

Rnd 7: Working behind petals made on rnd 6, sl st behind next sc from rnd 5, *5ch, 1sc around sc from rnd 5; rep from * around.

Rnd 8: Working behind petals made on rnd 7, sl st in first ch5-sp, ch3 (counts as 1 dc), (2dc ch2, 3dc) in same ch5-sp, 3dc in next ch5-sp, *(3dc, ch2, 3dc) in next ch5-sp, 3dc in next ch5-sp; rep from * twice more sl st to join.

Rnd 9: Ch3, (counts as 1dc), 2dc before next 3 dc group, 3dc in next sp before next 3 dc group, *(3dc ch2, 3dc) in corner sp, *3dc in space between next two 3 dc groups, (3dc, ch2, 3dc) in corner space; rep from * twice more, sl st to join.

Fasten off.

Join motifs into a row by sewing together through back loops.

With RS facing and 4mm/US6-G crochet hook, evenly distribute 61sc along long edge of motifs, turn.

Row 1: Ch1 (does not count as st), sc to end, turn.

Rep last row 3 more times.

Fasten off.

With RS facing, turn work and rejoin yarn to second long edge of motifs, with 4mm/US6-G crochet hook, evenly distribute 61sc along long edge of motifs, turn.

Complete as for Back from ** to **.

TO FINISH

Join Front to Back at shoulder working a seam along shoulder edge of 5 (5, 4, 4)cm/2 (2, 1½, 1½)in.

Sew side seams.

BOTTOM EDGING

With RS facing and 4mm/US6-G crochet hook, rejoin yarn to bottom edge of garment.

Work 3 rounds in sc around bottom edge, turn after each rnd.

ARMBANDS

With RS facing and 3.5mm/US4 crochet hook, rejoin yarn at top of side seam. Work 3 rounds in sc around armhole, turn after each rnd.

Rep for second armhole.

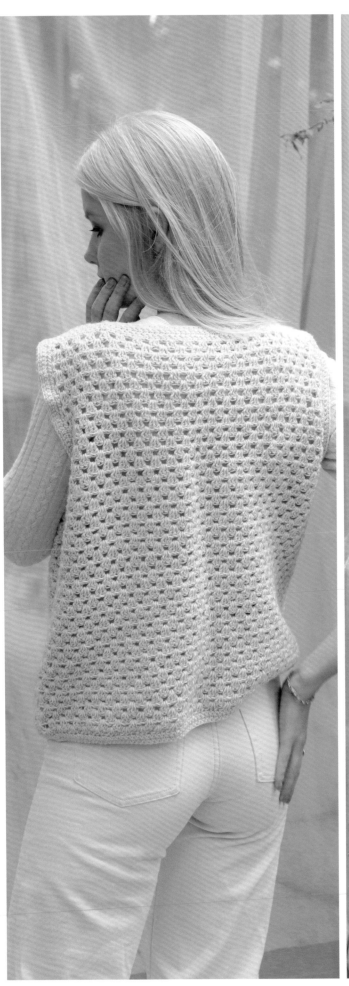

Loose
LEAF JUMPER
(with three quarter length sleeves)

This loose fitting garment is a casual every day piece but fun enough to still be the height of fashion. It has lovely three quarter length sleeves.

PATTERN BACKGROUND

This loose fitting garment is a casual every day piece but fun enough to still be the height of fashion. It has lovely three quarter length sleeves.

DIFFICULTY

 ★ ★ ★

MATERIALS

Scheepjes Skies Heavy, 100% Premium Blend Cotton, 100g/170m/186yds
Cirrostratus 106 x 5 (6, 7, 8) balls
4mm/US6-G and 5.5mm/US9-I crochet hooks

YARN ALTERNATIVES

You can use any Aran weight yarn that works to the same tension.

TENSION

16 sts and 8 rows measure approx 10 x 10cm/4 x 4in in pattern using 5.5mm/US9-I hook, or size required to obtain tension.

MEASUREMENTS

To Fit	S	M	L	XL
Actual bust approx				
	120	128	136	143 cm
	47	50	53½	56 in
Length approx				
	52	53	55	57 cm
	20½	21	21½	22½ in
Sleeve length				
	28	28	28	28 cm
	11	11	11	11 in

(Designed to be loose fitting/oversized.)

PATTERN STARTS

RIBBING (make 2 alike)

Using 5.5mm/US9-I hook, ch9.
Row 1: 1sc in 2nd ch from hook and in each ch to end, turn - 8sc.
Row 2: 1sc blo in each sc to end, turn - 8sc blo.
Rows 3-98 (104, 110, 116): Rep row 2.
Fasten off.

FRONT AND BACK (both alike)

Take one piece of ribbing, rejoin yarn and evenly distribute 98 (104, 110, 116)sc along row ends, turn.
Row 1: Ch3 (counts as first dc here and throughout), 1 (4, 7, 10)dc, ch2, miss 2 sc, * dc2tog, 3dc, dc2tog, ch2, miss 2 sc, 3dc in next sc, ch2, miss 2 sc, 9dc, ch2, miss 2 sc; rep from *3 more times, 2 (5, 8, 11)dc, turn.
Row 2: Ch3, 1 (4, 7, 10)dc, ch2, miss 2 ch, *dc2tog, 5dc, dc2tog, ch2, miss 2 ch, 2dc in next dc, 1dc, 2dc in next dc, ch2, miss 2 ch, dc2tog, 1dc, dc2tog, ch2, miss 2 ch; rep from * 3 more times, 2 (5, 8, 11)dc to end, turn.
Row 3: Ch3, 1 (4, 7, 10)dc, ch2, miss 2 ch, *dc3tog, ch2, miss 2 ch, 2dc in next dc, 3dc, 2dc in next dc, ch2, 3dc in ch2-sp, ch2, dc2tog, 3dc, dc2tog, ch2, miss 2 ch; rep from * 3 more times, 2 (5, 8, 11)dc to end, turn.
Row 4: Ch3, 1 (4, 7, 10)dc, ch2, miss 2 ch, *dc2tog, 1dc, dc2tog, ch2, miss 2 ch, 2dc in next dc, 1dc, 2dc in next dc, ch2, miss 2 ch, 2dc in next dc, 5dc, 2dc in next dc, ch2, miss (ch2, dc3tog, ch2); rep from * 3 more times 2 (5, 8, 11)dc to end, turn.
Row 5: Ch3, 1 (4, 7, 10)dc, ch2, miss 2 ch, *9dc, ch2, miss 2 ch, 2dc in next dc, 3dc, 2dc in next dc, ch2, miss 2 ch, dc3tog, ch2, miss 2 ch; rep from 3 more times, 2 (5, 8, 11) dc to end, turn.
Row 6: Ch3, 1 (4, 7, 10)dc, ch2, miss (2 ch, dc3tog, 2 ch), *2dc in next dc, 5dc, 2dc in next dc, ch2, miss 2 ch, dc2tog, 5dc, dc2tog, ch2, miss 2 ch; rep from * 3 more times, 2 (5, 8, 11)dc to end, turn.
Row 7: Ch3, 1 (4, 7, 10)dc, ch2, miss 2 ch, *dc2tog, 3dc, dc2tog, ch2, 3dc in ch2-sp, ch2, 9dc, ch2, miss 2 ch; rep from * 3 more times, 2 (5, 8, 11)dc to end, turn.
Row 8: Ch3, 1 (4, 7, 10)dc, ch2, miss 2 ch, *dc2tog, 5dc, dc2tog, ch2, miss 2 ch, 2dc in next dc, 1dc, 2dc in next dc, ch2, miss 2 ch, dc2tog, 1dc, dc2tog, ch2; rep from * 3 more times, 2 (5, 8, 11)dc to end, turn.
Row 9: Ch3, 1 (4, 7, 10)dc, ch2, miss 2 ch, *dc3tog, ch2, miss 2 ch, 2dc in next dc, 3dc, 2dc in next dc, ch2, 3dc in ch2-sp, ch2, dc2tog, 3dc, dc2tog, ch2, miss 2 ch; rep from * 3 more times, 2 (5, 8, 11)dc to end, turn.
Row 10: Ch3, 1 (4, 7, 10)dc, ch2, miss 2 ch, *dc2tog, 1dc, dc2tog, ch2, miss 2 ch, 2dc in next dc, 1dc, 2dc in next dc, ch2, miss 2 ch, 2dc in next dc, 5dc, 2dc in next dc, ch2, miss (2 ch, dc3tog, 2 ch); rep from * 3 more times, 2 (5, 8, 11)dc to end, turn.

Row 11: Ch3, 1 (4, 7, 10)dc, ch2, miss 2 ch, *9dc, ch2, miss 2 ch, 2dc in next dc, 3dc, 2dc in next dc, ch2, miss 2 ch, dc3tog, ch2; rep from * 3 more times, 2 (5, 8, 11)dc to end, turn.
Row 12: Ch3, 1 (4, 7, 10)dc, ch2, miss (2 ch, dc3tog, 2 ch), *2dc in next dc, 5dc, 2dc in next dc, ch2, miss 2 ch, dc2tog, 5dc, dc2tog, ch2, miss 2 ch; rep from * 3 more times, 2 (5, 8, 11)dc to end, turn.
Row 13: Ch3, 1 (4, 7, 10)dc, ch2, miss 2 ch, *dc2tog, 3dc, dc2tog, ch2, 3dc in ch2-sp, ch2, 9dc, ch2, miss 2 ch; rep from * 3 more times, 2 (5, 8, 11)dc to end, turn.
Rep rows 2 - 13 once more.
Rep rows 2 - 6 (6, 8, 10) once more.
Next row: Evenly distribute 98 (104, 110, 116)sc along top edge.
Next 2 rows: Ch1, 1sc in each st, turn.
Fasten off.

TO MAKE UP

Block Back and Front pieces.
Join Front to Back at shoulder joining 25 (28, 31, 34) sts on each side (see schematic).
Join sides seams leaving 18 (18, 19, 19)cm/7 (7, 7½, 7½)in open for arm hole.

SLEEVES (both alike)

Join yarn under arm at top of side seam, evenly distribute 50 (50, 54, 54)dc around armhole, sl st to join, turn.
Rows 2-22: 1dc in each st sl st to join, turn.
Change to 4mm/US6-G hook.
Rows 23-24: Ch1 (does not count as st), 1sc in each st around, sl st to join, turn.
Fasten off.

TO FINISH
Darn in ends.

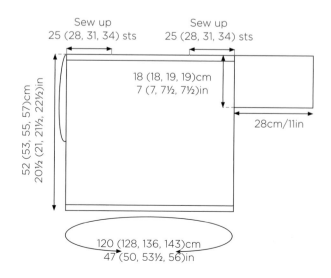

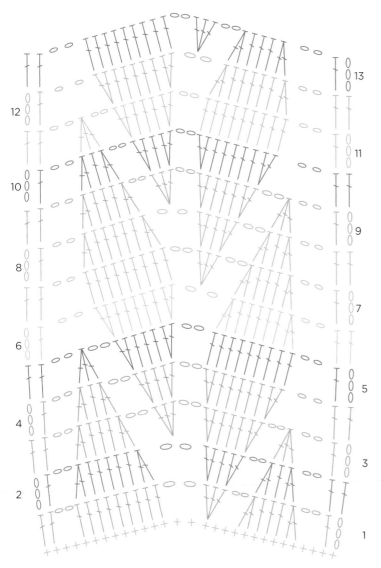

◯ **ch -** chain

✕ **sc -** single crochet

† **dc -** double crochet

⋀ **dc2tog -** double crochet two together

⋀ **dc3tog -** double crochet three together

Sunshine
SHRUG

This soft cuddly shrug is an easy garment to slip over the top of your favorite outfit. It has a beautiful soft texture and is simple to make once you have mastered the stitch.

DIFFICULTY

★ ★

MATERIALS

Scheepjes Eliza, 100% Polyester, 100g/230m/251yds
Gentle Apricot 214 x 6 (6, 7, 8) balls
US7/4.5mm crochet hook

YARN ALTERNATIVES

You can use any DK yarn that works to the same tension.

TENSION

Work 16 sts and 10 rows in pattern to measure approx 10 x 10cm/4 x 4in using US7/4.5mm hook

SPECIAL STITCHES

Fat Puff (FP): (yrh, insert hook, yrh, pull loop through to height of 1dc) five times, (11 loops on hook), yrh pull through all 11 loops, 1ch to secure.

MEASUREMENTS

To Fit	S	M	L	XL
Cuff edge to cuff edge				
	78	83	88	93 cm
(approx)	30¾	32¾	34¾	36¾ in
Nape to bottom edge				
	77	81	85	88 cm
(approx)	30¼	32	33½	34¾ in

PATTERN STARTS

MAIN PIECE

Using US7/4.5mm hook 115 (121, 127, 133)ch.

Row 1: 1sc in 2nd ch from hook, 1sc in each ch to end, turn - 114 (120, 126, 132) sts.

Row 2: Ch3, (counts as first dc), [1FP, ch 1, miss 1 sc] to end, ending with 1FP in last sc, turn.

Row 3: Ch4 (counts as 1dc, ch 1), [1FP in ch1-sp, ch 1] to last ch-sp, 1dc in top of t-ch, turn.

Row 4: Ch1 (does not count as st), 1sc in top off 1 dc of previous row, 1sc in each ch-sp and FP to end, 1sc in top of t-ch, turn.

Row 5: Ch3 (counts as 1 dc), 1dc in each sc to end, turn.

Row 6: Ch1, 1sc in each dc to end, turn.

Rows 7-73 (78, 83, 88): Rep rows 2-6 ending on a row 4. Fasten off.

CUFF EDGING

With RS facing, rejoin yarn to one short edge.
Working sc2tog 5 (4, 3, 2) times across row, evenly distribute 109 (116, 123, 130)sc along short edge.

Row 2: Ch1, 1sc in each dc to end, turn.

Row 3: Ch1, 1sc in each dc to end.
Fasten off.
Repeat for second short side.

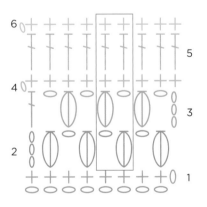

+ **sc** - single crochet

┬ **dc** - double crochet

⬭ **ch** - chain

⬯ **FP** - fat puff

▢ pattern repeat

FRONT EDGING

Fold garment with rows going vertically down body, join cuff edge A to cuff edge B (and similarly C to D) leaving a gap of 14 (16, 18, 20)cm/5½ (6¼, 7, 8)in for armholes (see schematic).

With RS facing, rejoin yarn at bottom edge of garment (indicated with red cross on schematic).

Rnd 1: Ch1 (does not count as st here and throughout), working into row ends work 238 (250, 262, 274)sc around entire edge of garment, sl st to first ch to join, turn.

Rnd 2: Ch 1, sc around, sl st to t-ch to join.
Rep last rnd a further 3 times.
Fasten off.

TO FINISH

Darn in ends.

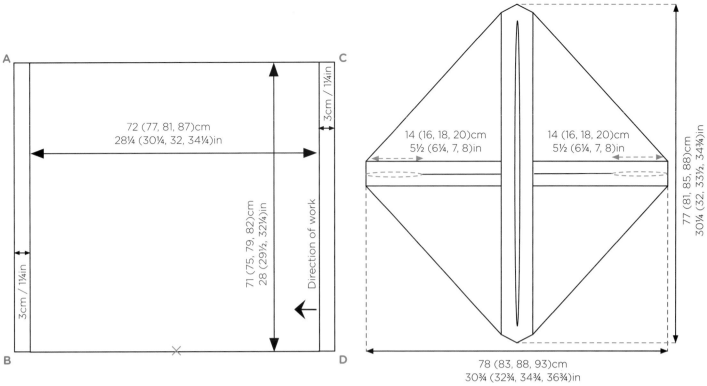

A

72 (77, 81, 87)cm
28¼ (30¼, 32, 34¼)in

C

3cm / 1¼in

71 (75, 79, 82)cm
28 (29½, 32¼)in

Direction of work

3cm / 1¼in

B

14 (16, 18, 20)cm
5½ (6¼, 7, 8)in

14 (16, 18, 20)cm
5½ (6¼, 7, 8)in

77 (81, 85, 88)cm
30¼ (32, 33½, 34¾)in

D

78 (83, 88, 93)cm
30¾ (32¾, 34¾, 36¾)in

Basket Stitch
CROPPED JACKET

This cropped cardigan, with its lovely texture, is so on trend, perfect with a pair of jeans or over the top of your favorite dress. It can be worn open or done up for a totally different look.

DIFFICULTY

★ ★ ★

MATERIALS

Scheepjes Merino Soft, 50% wool superwash merino, 25% acrylic, 25% microfiber, 50g/105m
Renoir 624 x 17 (19, 21, 23) balls
US4-E/3.5mm and US6-G/4mm hook
1 x 10mm button

YARN ALTERNATIVES

You can use any DK yarn that works to same tension.

TENSION

Work 20 sts and 13 rows in basket weave pattern to 10 x 10cm/4 x 4in using US6-G/4mm hook or size required to obtain tension.

SPECIAL STITCHES

Front Post Double Crochet (fpdc): Yrh, insert hook from front to back to front around vertical post of next stitch, yrh, pull up a loop, (yrh, pull through 2 loops) twice.

Back Post Double Crochet (bpdc): Yrh, insert hook from back to front to back around vertical post of next stitch, yrh, pull up a loop, (yrh, pull through 2 loops) twice.

MEASUREMENTS

SIZE	S	M	L	XL
Actual bust				
	94	102	110	118 cm
	37	40	43¼	46½ in
Shoulder to shoulder				
	47	51	55	59 cm
	18½	20	21½	23¼ in
Length to underarm				
	23	23	27	27 cm
	9	9	10½	10½ in
Length to shoulder				
	40	40	46	46 cm
	15¾	15¾	18	18 in
Sleeve length				
	42	42	45	48
	16½	16½	17¾	19

PATTERN STARTS

BACK

Using US6-G/4mm hook, ch95 (103, 111, 119).
Row 1: 1dc in 3rd ch from hook, 1dc in each ch to end, turn - 94 (102, 110, 118) sts.
Row 2: Ch2 (counts as first st), 4fpdc, [4bpdc, 4fpdc] to last st, 1dc, turn.
Row 3: Ch2 (counts as first st), 4bpdc, [4fpdc, 4bpdc] to last st, 1dc, turn.
Row 4: Rep row 3.
Row 5: Rep row 2.
Rows 2 to 5 form Basket Weave Patt and are repeated.
Rows 6-52 (52, 60, 60): Rep rows 2-5.
Fasten off.

FRONTS (both alike)

Using US6-G/4mm hook, ch55 (59, 63, 67).
Row 1: 1dc in 3rd ch from hook, 1dc in each ch to end, turn - 54 (58, 62, 66) sts.

Sizes S and L only
Rows 2-52 (60): Work in Basket Weave Patt as for Back.
Fasten off.

Sizes M and XL only
Row 2: Ch2 (counts as first st), [4bpdc, 4fpdc] to last st, 1dc, turn.
Row 3: Rep row 2.
Row 4: Ch2 (counts as first st), [4fpdc, 4bpdc] to last st, 1dc, turn.
Row 5: Rep row 4.
Rows 2 to 5 form Basket Weave Patt and are repeated.
Rows 6-52 (60): Rep rows 2-5.

SLEEVES (both alike)

Using US6-G/4mm hook, ch56 (56, 64, 64) sl st to form a ring.
Work in rnds as folls:

Rnd 1: Ch3 (counts first dc), 1dc in each ch around - 56 (56, 64, 64) sts.
Rnd 2: Ch2 (does not count as st), [4fpdc, 4bpdc] around, sl st in first fpdc, turn.
Rnd 3: Rep rnd 2.
Rnd 4: Ch2 (does not count as st), [4bpdc, 4fpdc] around, sl st in first bpdc, turn.
Rnd 5: Rep rnd 4.
Rows 2 to 5 form Basket Weave Patt and are repeated.
Rnds 6-52 (52, 56, 60): Rep rnds 2-5.
Fasten off.

CUFFS

Working into other side of starting ch, work [6sc, sc2tog] around, sl st to join - 49 (49, 56, 56) sts.
Change to US4-E/3.5mm hook.
Rnds 2-3: Ch1, 1sc in each st around, sl st to join, turn.
Rnd 4: [5sc, sc2tog] around - 42 (42, 48, 48) sts.
Fasten off.

TO MAKE UP

Join at shoulders only sewing 16 (16, 18, 18)cm in from outside edge of shoulder and leaving remainder to flap. Sew in sleeves. Join under arm and sleeve seam.

NECKBAND

With RS facing and US6-G/4mm rejoin yarn to neck edge of right front.
Row 1: Ch1, 1sc in each st around neck, 5ch, sl st to last sc to form button hole.
Fasten off.

TO FINISH

Sew on button. Sew in ends.

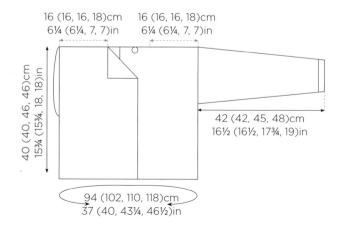

16 (16, 16, 18)cm
6¼ (6¼, 7, 7)in

16 (16, 16, 18)cm
6¼ (6¼, 7, 7)in

40 (40, 46, 46)cm
15¾ (15¾, 18, 18)in

42 (42, 45, 48)cm
16½ (16½, 17¾, 19)in

94 (102, 110, 118)cm
37 (40, 43¼, 46½)in

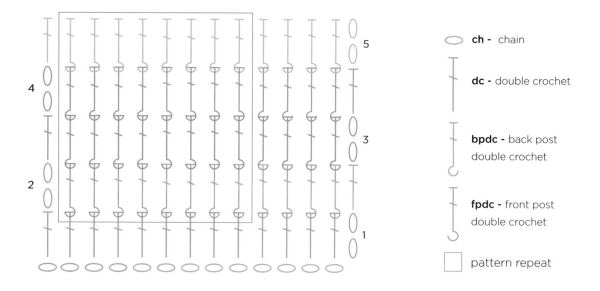

⬭	**ch -**	chain
⊺	**dc -**	double crochet
	bpdc -	back post double crochet
	fpdc -	front post double crochet
☐	pattern repeat	

Read odd rows from L to R and even rows from R to L

Chart shows pattern worked over multiple of 8 sts + 6.

NB: When working Fronts, sizes M and XL are worked over multiple of 8 sts + 2.

Boho
FRINGED DRESS

This A-line dress with fringe detail is absolutely perfect for a casual shop-ping trip, a day at the beach or even a festival. Its pretty fringe detail means it's a really fun addition to your summer wardrobe.

DIFFICULTY

★ ★

MATERIALS

Scheepjes Catona Denim 100% cotton, 50g/125m/136yds
10 (11, 12, 13) balls in shade 102
4mm/USG-6 crochet hook

YARN ALTERNATIVES

You can use any 4 ply weight yarn that works to the same tension.

TENSION

18 sts x 10 rows in pattern to measure 10 x 10cm/4 x 4in using 4mm/USG-6 crochet hook

MEASUREMENTS

SIZE	S	M	L	XL
Actual bust approx				
	85	92	103	112 cm
	34	36	40½	44 in
Length (before fringing) approx				
	75	75	80	80 cm
	29½	29½	31½	31½ in

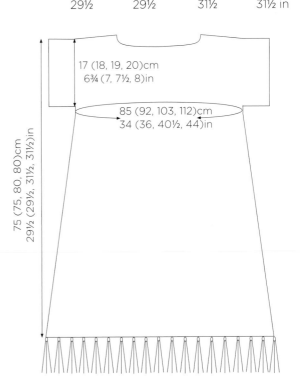

17 (18, 19, 20)cm
6¾ (7, 7½, 8)in

85 (92, 103, 112)cm
34 (36, 40½, 44)in

75 (75, 80, 80)cm
29½ (29½, 31½, 31½)in

BACK

Using 4mm/USG-6 hook ch104 (112, 120. 128).

Row 1: 1sc in 2nd ch from hook and in each ch to end, turn - 103 (111, 119, 127)sc.

Row 2: Ch3, (counts as 1dc here and throughout) 1dc in each st to end, turn.

Row 3: Ch3, dc2tog, dc to end, turn - 102 (110, 118, 126)dc.

Row 4: Ch3, dc2tog, dc to end, turn - 101 (109, 117, 125)dc.

Row 5: Ch3, dc to end, turn.

Row 6: Ch4 (counts as 1dc and 1 ch), [miss 1 dc, 1dc, ch1] to end work-ing 1dc in top of 3 ch, turn.

Row 7: Ch3, 1dc in each ch1-sp and dc to end, work last dc in 3rd of ch 4, turn.

Row 8: Ch3, dc2tog, dc to end, turn - 100 (108, 116, 124) dc.

Row 9: Ch3, dc2tog, dc to end, turn - 99 (107, 115, 123)dc.

Row 10: Ch3, dc to end, turn.

Row 11: Ch4 (counts as 1dc and 1 ch), miss 1 dc, 1dc in next dc, [ch1, miss 1 dc, 1dc in next dc] to end, turn.

Rows 12 - 66: Rep rows 7 - 11 a further 11 times - 77 (85, 93, 101)sc.

Row 67: Ch3, 1dc in each ch1-sp and dc to end, work last dc in 3rd of ch 4, turn.

Rows 68 - 70: Ch3, dc to end, turn.

Row 71: Ch4 (counts as 1dc and 1 ch), miss 1 dc, [1dc, ch1, 1dc in next dc] to end.

Rep last 5 rows 0 (0, 1, 1) more times.

Row 72 (72, 77, 77): Rep row 7. **

Rows 73 (73, 78, 78) - 75 (75, 80, 80): Ch3, dc to end, turn.

Fasten off.

FRONT

Work as for Back to **.

Shape Left Neck

Row 1: Ch3, 21 (24, 27, 30)dc, dc2tog, turn - 23 (26, 29, 32) sts.

Row 2: Ch3, dc2tog, 21 (24, 27, 30)dc, turn - 22 (25, 28, 31) sts.

Row 3: Ch3, 19 (22, 25, 28)dc, dc2tog, turn - 21 (24, 27, 30) sts.

Row 4: Ch3, dc2tog, 19 (22, 25, 28)dc - 20 (23, 26, 29) sts.

Fasten off

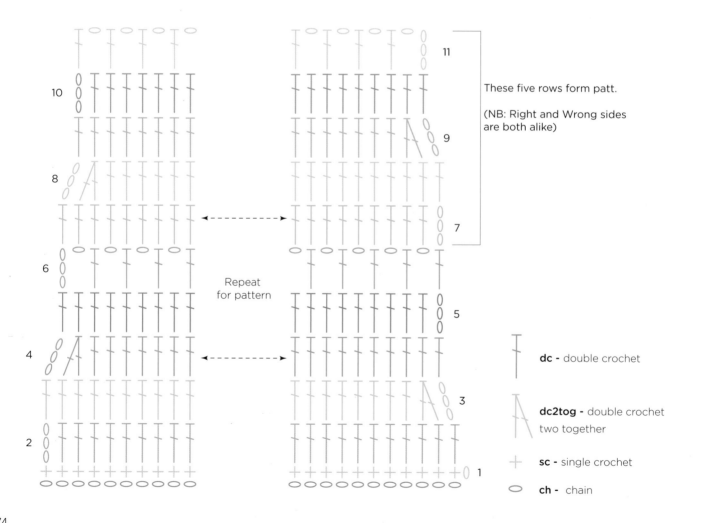

These five rows form patt.

(NB: Right and Wrong sides are both alike)

dc - double crochet

dc2tog - double crochet two together

sc - single crochet

ch - chain

Shape Right Neck

Row 1: Rejoin yarn 24 (27, 30, 33) sts in from row end, dc2tog, 22 (25, 28, 31)dc -23 (26, 29, 32) sts.

Row 2: Ch3, 20 (23, 26, 29)dc, dc2tog, turn - 22 (25, 28, 31) sts.

Row 3: Ch3, dc2tog, 20 (23, 26, 29)dc, turn - 21 (24, 27, 30) sts.

Row 4: Ch3, 18 (21, 24, 27)dc, dc2tog - 20 (23, 26, 29) sts.
Fasten off.

TO MAKE UP

Sew Front to Back at shoulders. Sew side seams leaving 17 (18, 19, 20)cm/6¾ (7, 7½, 8)in gap for armhole.

SLEEVES (both alike)

Join yarn at top of side seam at under arm.

Using 4mm/USG-6 crochet hook, evenly distribute 58 (62, 66, 70)dc around armhole, turn.

Row 2: Ch3, 1dc in each st around, sl st to top of ch 3, turn.

Rows 3-4: Rep row 2.

Row 5: Ch4 (counts as 1dc and 1 ch), miss 1 dc, [1dc in next dc, ch1, miss 1 dc] around, sl st to 3rd of ch 4, turn.

Row 6: Ch3, 1 dc in each dc and ch1-sp around, sl st to top of ch 3, turn.

Rows 7-8: Rep row 2.

Row 9: 1sc in each st around, sl st to first sc.
Fasten off.

FINISHING

Work 2 rows in sc around neck edge.
Darn in ends.
Make 52 (56, 60, 64) tassels to desired length and attached to bottom of dress after approx every fourth st around.

Lace Back
JUMPER

This statement lace back jumper is the perfect addition to any wardrobe. Its delicate lace design makes it perfect to pop over your favorite dress or to warm up on a summer's eve.

DIFFICULTY

★ ★ ★

MATERIALS

Scheepjes Whirligigette, 20% alpaca, 80% virgin wool, 100g/215m/235yds
Blue 255 x 5 (6, 7, 8) balls
4mm/USG-6, 4.5mm/US7, and 5mm/US8 crochet hooks

YARN ALTERNATIVES

You can use any DK weight yarn that works to the same tension.

TENSION

17 sts x 8 rows in double crochet to measure 10 x 10cm/4 x 4in using 4.5mm/US7 hook or size required to obtain tension.

MEASUREMENTS

To fit	S	M	L	XL
Actual bust approx				
	100	112	123	135 cm
	39½	44	48½	53 in
Length to shoulder approx				
	52	52	56	56 cm
	20½	20½	22	22 in
Sleeve seam approx				
	52	52	52	52 cm
	20½	20½	20½	20½ in

SPECIAL ABBREVIATIONS

Shell = work 5dc all in next st
Dc2tog = yrh, insert hook, yrh, pull through (3 loops on hook), yrh, pull through 2 loops, yrh, insert hook in same st/space, yrh, pull through (4 loops on hook), [yrh, pull through 2 loops] twice
Inc = increase
Sc blo = single crochet into back loop only

PATTERN STARTS

FRONT

WELT

Using 5mm/US8 hook, ch13.

Row 1: 1sc in 2nd ch from hook and in each ch to end, turn - 12sc.

Rows 2-85 (95, 105, 115): Ch1, sc blo to end, turn. Fasten off.

Using 5mm/US8 hook, evenly distribute 85 (95, 105, 115) sc along long edge of welt. **

Rows 1-18: Ch3 (counts as 1dc), 1dc in each st to end, turn - 85 (95, 105, 115)dc.

Change to 4.5mm/US7 hook.

Rows 19-39 (39, 45, 45): Rep row 1.

SHAPE NECK

Row 1: Ch3, 20 (25, 30, 35)dc, dc2tog, turn - 22 (27, 32, 37)dc.

Row 2: Dc2tog, 20 (25, 30, 35)dc, turn - 21 (26, 31, 36)dc.

Row 3: Ch3, 18 (23, 28, 33)dc, dc2tog, turn - 20 (25, 30, 35)dc.

Fasten off.

With RS facing, leaving center 39 sts free for neck, rejoin yarn in next st and work dc2tog, 21 (26, 31, 36)dc, turn - 22 (27, 32, 37)dc

Row 2: Ch3, 19 (24, 29, 34)dc, dc2tog, turn - 21 (26, 31, 36)dc.

Row 3: Dc2tog, 19 (24, 29, 33) dc - 20 (25, 30, 35)dc.

Fasten off.

BACK

Work as for Front to ** - 85 (95, 105, 115)sc.

Row 1: Ch3 (counts as 1dc), 19 (24, 29, 34)dc, *ch3, miss 2 sc, 1sc in next st, ch3, miss 3 sc, Shell in next st, ch3, miss 3 sc, 1sc in next st, ch3, miss 2 sc, 3dc; rep from * twice more, 17 (22, 27, 32)dc, turn.

Row 2: Ch3, 19 (24, 29, 34)dc, *ch3, 1dc in first dc of Shell, (ch1, 1dc) in each of next 4 dc, ch3, 1dc in each of next 3 dc; rep from * twice more, 17 (22, 27, 32)dc, turn.

Row 3: Ch3, 19 (24, 29, 34)dc, *ch3, dc2tog in next ch1-sp, (ch2, dc2tog) in each of next three ch2-sps, ch3, 1dc in each of next 3 dc; rep from * twice more, 17 (22, 27, 32)dc, turn.

Row 4: Ch3, 19 (24, 29, 34)dc, *ch4, dc2tog in first ch2-sp, (ch1, dc2tog) in each of next two ch2-sps, ch4, 1dc in each of next 3 dc; rep from * twice more, 17 (22, 27, 32) dc, turn.

Row 5: Ch3, 19 (24, 29, 34)dc, *ch5, dc2tog in first ch1-sp, ch1, dc2tog in next ch1-sp, ch5, 1dc in each of next 3 dc; rep from * twice more, 17 (22, 27, 32)dc, turn.

Row 6: Ch3, 19 (24, 29, 34)dc, *ch6, dc2tog in ch1-sp, ch6, 1dc in each of next 3 dc; rep from * twice more, 17 (22, 27, 32)dc, turn.

Row 7: Ch3, 19 (24, 29, 34)dc, *(ch3, 1sc, ch3) in ch6-sp, Shell in top of dc2tog, (ch3, 1sc, ch3) in next ch6-sp, 1dc in each of next 3 dc; rep from * twice more, 17 (22, 27, 32)dc, turn.

Rows 8-12: Rep rows 2-6.

Rows 13-42 (42, 47, 47): Rep rows 2-6 changing to 4.5mm/US7 hook from row 19 onwards.

Sizes L and XL only
Row 48: Rep row 2.
Fasten off.

SLEEVES (both alike)

CUFF

Using 4.5mm/US7 hook, ch13.

Row 1: 1sc in 2nd ch from hook and in each ch to end, turn - 12sc.

Rows 2-29 (29, 33, 33): Ch1, sc blo to end, turn. Fasten off.

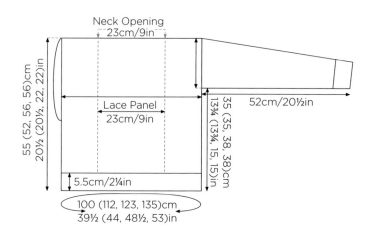

SLEEVES

Row 1: Evenly distribute 31 (31, 35, 35)sc along one long edge of cuff.

Row 2 (inc): Ch3 (counts as 1dc here and throughout) 1dc in same sp, 8 (8, 10, 10)dc, *ch3, miss 2 sc, 1sc in next st, ch3, miss 3 sc, Shell in next st, ch3, miss 3 sc, 1sc in next st, ch3, miss 2 sc, 8 (8, 10, 10)dc, 2dc in last st, turn - 33 (33, 37, 37) sts.

Row 3 (inc): Ch3, 1dc in same sp, 9 (9, 11, 11)dc, *ch3, 1dc in first dc of Shell, (ch1, 1dc) in each of next 4 dc, ch3, 9 (9, 11, 11)dc, 2dc in last st, turn - 35 (35, 37, 37) sts.

Row 4 (inc): Ch3, 1dc in same sp, 10 (10, 12, 12)dc, ch3, [dc2tog in next ch1-sp, ch2] three times, dc2tog in next ch-sp, ch3, 10 (10, 12, 12)dc, 2dc in last dc, turn - 37 (37, 39, 39) sts.

Row 5: Ch3, 11 (11, 13, 13)dc, ch4, [dc2tog in next ch2-sp, ch1] twice, dc2tog in next ch2-sp, 4ch, 12 (12, 14, 14)dc, turn.

Row 6 (inc): Ch3, 1dc in same sp, 11 (11, 13, 13,)dc, ch5, dc2tog in next ch1-sp, ch1, dc2tog in next ch1-sp, ch5, 11 (11, 13, 13)dc, 2dc in last dc, turn - 39 (39, 41, 41)dc.

Row 7: Ch3, 12 (12, 14, 14)dc, ch6, dc2tog in ch1-sp, ch6, 13 (13, 15, 15)dc, turn.

Row 8: Ch3, 1dc in same sp, 12 (12, 14, 14)dc, ch3, 1sc in ch6-sp, Shell in top of dc2tog, ch3, 1sc in ch6-sp, 12 (12, 14, 14)dc, 2dc in last dc, turn - 41 (41, 43, 43)dc.

Rows 9-14: Rep rows 3-8.

Rows 15-19: Rep rows 9-13.

Rows 20-37: Rep rows 8-13 but do not work incs as start and ends of rows.

Row 38: Ch1, 1sc in next 20 (20, 22, 22)dc, 5sc in ch6-sp, 1sc in top of dc2tog, 5sc in ch6-sp, 1sc in next 20 (20, 22, 22)dc.

Fasten off.

TO FINISH

Sew sleeve seam.

Sew front to back along shoulders.

Sew up along sides leaving open approx 17 (17, 18, 18)cm for armhole.

Sew in sleeves.

Using 4mm/USG-6 hook work 2 rows in sc around neck edge.

Darn in ends.

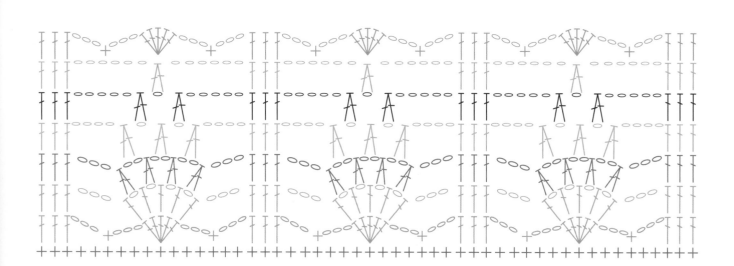

○ **ch -** chain   + **sc -** single crochet | **dc -** double crochet   ⋀ **dc2tog -** double crochet two together

Diamond
JUMPER DRESS

This oversized snuggly jumper dress is just the job to cuddle up in front of a nice warm fire. Its oversized fit and bell sleeves make it a really beautiful piece.

DIFFICULTY

MATERIALS
Scheepjes Merino Soft, 50% wool superwash Merino, 25% microfiber, 25% acrylic, 50g/105m/115yds
Michelangelo 603 x 18 (19, 22, 24) balls
4mm/USG-6 and 4.5mm/US7 crochet hooks

YARN ALTERNATIVES
You can use any DK weight yarn that works to the same tension.

TENSION
19 sts and 10 rows over double crochet to 10 x 10cm/4 x 4in using 4mm/USG-6 crochet hook or size required to obtain tension.

MEASUREMENTS

SIZE	S	M	L	XL
Actual bust approx				
	99	108	116	124 cm
	39	42½	45½	48¾ in
Length to shoulder approx				
	74	74	74	74 cm
	29	29	29	29 in
Sleeve length				
	43	43	45	45 cm
	17	17	17¾	17¾ in

PATTERN STARTS

BACK

RIBBING

4mm/USG-6 hook, ch17.

Row 1: 1sc in 2nd ch from hook and in each ch to end, turn - 16sc.

Rows 2-94 (102, 110, 118): 1sc in blo of each sc to end, turn.**

MAIN BODY

Turn and work along row ends of ribbing, using 4.5mm/US7 hook, evenly distribute 94 (102, 110, 118)sc to end, turn.

Rows 1-35: Ch3 (counts as first dc), 1dc in each st to end, turn.

Change to 4mm/USG-6 hook.

Rows 35-69: As row 1.
Fasten off.

FRONT

Work as for Back to **.

MAIN BODY

Turn and work along row ends of ribbing, using 4.5mm/US7 hook, evenly distribute 94 (102, 110, 118)sc to end, turn.

Row 1 (RS): Ch3 (counts as first dc here and throughout), 5 (1, 5, 1)dc, ch1, miss 1 st, work Chart row 1 to last 7 (3, 7, 3) sts, dc to end, turn.

This row sets position of Chart.

Continue working from Chart as folls:
Rows 3-35: Follow Chart.
Change to 4mm/USG-6 hook.
Rows 36-66: Follow Chart.

SHAPE LEFT NECK

Row 1 (Chart row 3) (RS): Ch3, patt across next 29 (33, 37, 41) sts, turn - 30 (34, 38, 42) sts.
Working on these 30 (34, 38, 42) sts only and keeping patt correct, work another two rows in patt.
Fasten off.

SHAPE RIGHT NECK

With RS facing Re join yarn 30 (34, 38, 42) sts in from end leaving center 34 sts unworked in all sizes.
Working on these 30 (34, 38, 42) sts only work from Chart.
Rows 2 and 3: Work from Chart to end.
Fasten off.

TO MAKE UP

Join at shoulders.
Join sides leaving 17 (17, 22.5, 22.5)cm/6¾ (6¾, 9, 9)in gap for armholes.

SLEEVES (both alike)

RIBBING

Using 4.5mm/US7, ch17.
Row 1: 1sc in 2nd ch from hook and in each ch to end, turn - 16sc.
Rows 2-35 (35, 40, 40): 1sc in blo of each sc to end, turn.
Turn and work along row ends of ribbing, evenly distribute 35 (35, 40, 40)sc to end, turn.
Rnd 1: Ch3 (counts as 1dc), 1dc in same st, 2dc in each sc to end, sl st to join, turn.
Rnds 2-16: Ch3, dc to end, sl st to join, turn.
Rnd 17: Ch3, 7dc, dc2tog, [8dc, dc2tog] around, sl st to join, turn.
Rnds 18-40 (40, 42, 42): Ch3, dc to end, sl st to join, turn.
Fasten off.

NECKBAND

(All sizes)
With 4mm/USG-6 hook, join yarn at back of neck, evenly distribute 84sc around neck, sl st to join, turn.
Rnd 1: 1dc in each sc around, sl st to join, turn.
Rnd 2: Ch3, [1fpdc, 1bpdc] around, sl st to join, turn.
Rnd 3: Ch3, [1bpdc, 1fpdc] around, sl st to join, turn
Rnds 5-18: Rep rows 2 and 3.
Fasten off.

TO FINISH

Sew in Sleeves.
Darn in loose ends.

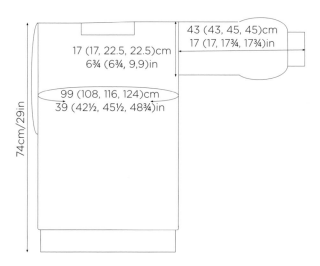

Diamond Dress Chart

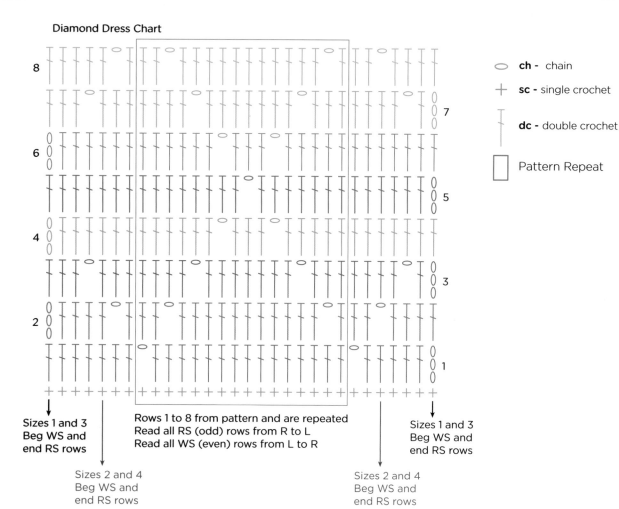

ch - chain

sc - single crochet

dc - double crochet

☐ Pattern Repeat

Sizes 1 and 3
Beg WS and
end RS rows

Rows 1 to 8 from pattern and are repeated
Read all RS (odd) rows from R to L
Read all WS (even) rows from L to R

Sizes 1 and 3
Beg WS and
end RS rows

Sizes 2 and 4
Beg WS and
end RS rows

Sizes 2 and 4
Beg WS and
end RS rows

Textured Roll
NECK PONCHO

This lightly textured roll neck poncho is easier than it looks.
Constructed from simple motifs to give a really wonderful
look, its chunky style yarn and roll neck will keep you all warm
and snuggly.

DIFFICULTY

★ ★

MATERIALS

**Scheepjes Chunky Monkey Anti Piling, 100% Premium
acrylic, 100g/116m/127yds**
Heather 1724 x 10 (13) balls
5.5mm/US9-I crochet hook

YARN ALTERNATIVES

You can use any Aran or chunky weight yarn that works
to the same tension.

TENSION

Size S/M Motif measures approx 20cm/8in
Size L/XL Motif measures approx 23.5cm/9¼in

SPECIAL STITCHES

Puff: (yrh, insert hook, yrh, pull up a loop to height of a
dc) three times, (7 loops on hook), yrh, pull through all
7 loops, ch1 to close.

Beginning Puff (BegPuff): ch3, *yrh, insert hook, yrh, pull
through loop to the height of a dc stitch; rep from * once
more (5 loops on hook), yrh pull through all 5 loops, ch1
to close.

MEASUREMENTS

SIZE	S/M	L/XL
Length from back neck approx		
	75	86 cm
	29½	34 in
Cuff edge to cuff edge approx		
	92	105 cm
	36¼	41¼ in

PATTERN STARTS

MOTIF (make 16)

Using 5.5mm/US9-I hook, ch6, sl st to form a ring.

Rnd 1: Ch3 (counts as first part of Puff) (yrh, insert hook in ring, yrh, pull up a loop to height of 1 dc) twice, (5 loops on hook), yrh pull through all 5 loops, ch1 to close, ch3, 1Puff, ch1, [1Puff, ch3, 1Puff, ch1] three times, sl st to top of ch 3 to join.

Rnd 2: Sl st in to ch3-sp, *(1Puff, ch3, 1Puff) in corner ch3-sp, ch2, 3dc in ch1-sp, ch2; rep from * 3 more times, sl st to first Puff to join.

Rnd 3: Sl st to corner ch3-sp, *(1Puff, ch3, 1Puff) in corner ch3-sp, ch2, 2dc in ch2-sp, 1dc in each dc to next ch2-sp, 2dc in ch2-sp, ch2; rep from * 3 more times, sl st to first Puff to join.

Rnds 4 - 6 (7): Rep rnd 3.
Fasten off.

HALF MOTIF (make 1)

Using 5.5mm/US9-I hook, ch6, sl st to form a ring.

Rnd 1: Ch3 (counts as first part of Puff) (yrh, insert hook in ring, yrh, pull up a loop to height of 1 dc) twice, (5 loops on hook), yrh pull through all 5 loops, ch1 to close, ch1, 1Puff, ch3, 1Puff, ch1, 1Puff, turn.

Rnd 2: Ch3 (counts as first part of Puff) (yrh, insert hook in top of Puff, yrh, pull up a loop to height of 1 dc) twice, (5 loops on hook), yrh pull through all 5 loops, ch1 to close, ch2, 3dc in ch1-sp, ch2, (1Puff, ch3, 1Puff) in ch3-sp, ch2, 3dc in ch1-sp, ch2, 1Puff in top of last Puff, turn.

Rnd 3: Ch3 (counts as first part of Puff) (yrh, insert hook in top of Puff, yrh, pull up a loop to height of 1 dc) twice, (5 loops on hook), yrh pull through all 5 loops, ch1 to close, ch2, 2dc in ch2-sp, 1dc in each dc to next ch2-sp, 2dc in ch2-sp, ch2, (1Puff, ch3, 1Puff) in ch3-sp, ch2, 2dc in ch2-sp, 1dc in each dc to next ch2-sp, 2dc in ch2-sp, ch2, 1Puff in top of last Puff, turn.

Rnds 4 - 6 (7): Rep rnd 3.
Fasten off.

TO MAKE UP

Block squares and join as directed in schematic.

POLO NECK

Join yarn in center of Half Motif at back of garment and evenly distribute 84 (92)dc around neck, sl st to join, TURN.

Row 1: [1fpdc, 1bpdc] around, sl st to join, turn.
Row 2: [1bpdc, 1fpdc] around, sl st to join, turn.
Rows 3-20 (22): Rep rows 1 -2.
Fasten off.

Edging: Join yarn anywhere on back of poncho, work 4 rows of sc around garment, sl st to join and turn after every row.

TO FINISH

Darn in ends.

○ **ch -** chain   **dc -** double crochet   puff stitch   beg puff

● **sl st -** slip stitch

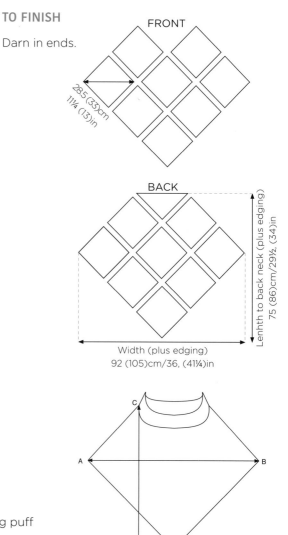

FRONT

28.5 (33)cm
11¼ (13)in

BACK

Lenth to back neck (plus edging)
75 (86)cm/29½, (34)in

Width (plus edging)
92 (105)cm/36, (41¼)in

The JOSIE TOP

This is a lovely little top with a slight crop. Its boxy style and pretty detail make it a staple piece of your wardrobe.

DIFFICULTY

★ ★ ★

MATERIALS

Scheepjes Merino Soft, 50% wool superwash Merino, 25% microfibre, 25% acrylic
8 (9, 10, 11) balls in 621 Picasso
4mm/US5-G crochet hook

YARN ALTERNATIVES

You can use any DK weight yarn that works to the same tension.

TENSION

19 sts x 10 rows in double crochet to measure 10 x 10cm/4 x 4in using 4mm/US6-G hook of size required to obtain tension.

MEASUREMENTS

SIZE	S	M	L	XL
Actual bust approx				
	102	115	128	140 cm
	40	45¼	50½	55 in
Length				
	47	47	51	51 cm
	18½	18½	20	20 in

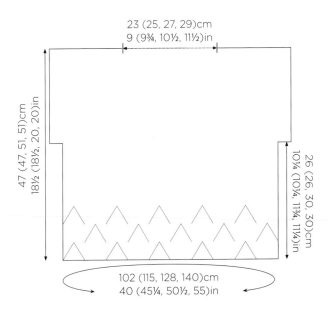

23 (25, 27, 29)cm
9 (9¾, 10½, 11½)in

47 (47, 51, 51)cm
18½ (18½, 20, 20)in

26 (26, 30, 30)cm
10¼ (10¼, 11¾, 11¼)in

102 (115, 128, 140)cm
40 (45¼, 50½, 55)in

BACK and FRONT (both alike)

Using 4mm/US6-G hook, 98 (110, 122, 134)ch.

Row 1: 1sc in 2nd ch from hook and in each ch to end, turn - 97 (109, 121, 133)sc.

Row 2: Ch3 (counts as 1 dc here and throughout), 4dc, miss 3 sc, ch3, *9dc, ch3, miss 3 sc; rep from * to last 5 sts, 5dc to end, turn.

Row 3: Ch3, 3dc, miss next dc, ch3, 1dc in ch3-sp, ch3, miss next dc, *7dc, miss next dc, ch3, 1dc in ch3-sp, ch3, miss next dc; rep from * to last 4 sts, 4dc, turn.

Row 4: Ch3, 2dc, ch5, miss next dc, 1dc in next dc, miss next dc, ch5, *5dc, ch5, miss next dc, 1dc in next dc, miss next dc, 5ch; rep from * to last 3 sts, 3dc, turn.

Row 5: Ch3, 1dc, ch5, miss next dc, 1dc in next dc, miss next dc, ch5, *3dc, ch5, miss next dc, 1dc in next dc, miss next dc, ch5; rep from * to last 2 sts, 2dc, turn.

Row 6: Ch8 (counts as 1dc and 5 ch here and throughout) miss 1 dc and first ch5-sp, 1dc in next dc, ch5, miss next dc, 1dc in next dc, *ch5, miss next dc, 1dc in next dc, miss next dc, ch5, 1dc in next dc; rep from * to end, turn.

Row 7: Ch4 (counts as 1dc and 1 ch), *4dc in ch5-sp, 1dc in next dc, 4dc in next ch5-sp, ch3; rep from * to last st, ch1, 1dc, turn.

Row 8: Ch6 (counts as 1dc, 3 ch), miss 1 ch and next dc, 7dc, *ch3, 1dc in ch3-sp, ch3, miss next dc, 7dc; rep from * to last 9 sts, miss next dc, 7dc, ch3, 1dc, turn.

Row 9: Ch8, miss ch3-sp, *miss next dc, 5dc, ch5, miss next dc, 1dc in next dc, ch5; rep from * to last 7 sts, miss next dc, 5dc, ch5, 1dc in 3rd of 6 ch, turn.

Row 10: Ch8, *miss next dc, 3dc, ch5, miss next dc, 1dc in next dc, ch5; rep from * to last 5 sts, miss next dc, 3dc, ch5, miss 1dc, 1dc in 3rd of 8 ch, turn.

Row 11: Ch8, miss ch5-sp and next dc, 1dc, ch5, miss next dc, 1dc in next dc, *ch5, miss next dc, 1dc, ch5, miss next dc, 1dc; rep from * to end, turn.

Row 12: Evenly distribute 97 (109, 121, 133)dc in each st and ch-sp across row, turn.

Rows 13-25 (25, 29, 29): Ch3 (counts as first dc), dc to end, turn.

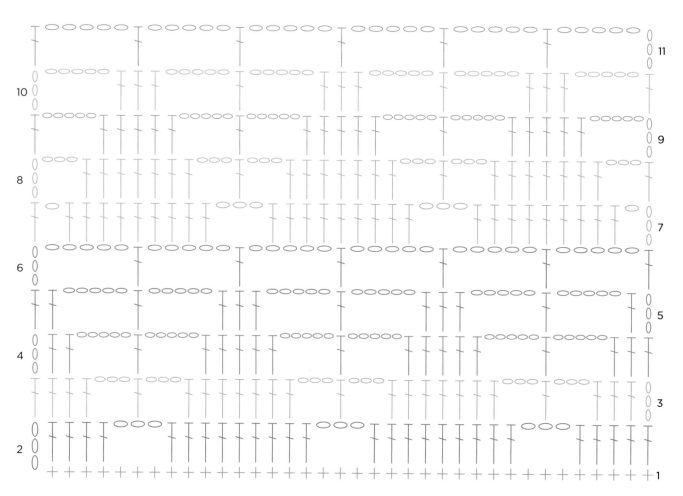

⌒ **ch -** chain   ┼ **sc -** single crochet   ┬ **dc -** double crochet

Row 26 (26, 30, 30): 8ch, 1dc in 3rd ch from hook, 1dc in each of next 4 ch (adding 6 sts), dc to end, do not turn, but with a separate piece of yarn, work 6ch and join to end of row, work 1dc in each of these 6 ch, turn - 109 (121, 133, 145) dc.

Rows 27 (27, 31, 31) - 47 (47, 51, 51): Ch3, dc to end, turn.

Fasten off.

TO FINISH

Join Front to Back at shoulders leaving 23 (25, 27, 29)cm gap in center for neck.

Join side and under arm seams.

EDGING

Work 1 row in sc around each armhole.
Fasten off.

Sew in ends.

Thank You

It is with total gratitude and amazement that I write these words, creating this book has been an absolute joy but it wouldn't have been possible without some fabulous people around me.

Firstly, I'd like to thank Kader and Ayhan for giving me this opportunity; the initial email came totally out of the blue whilst on holiday in Cape Verde, and was a complete surprise, I was so flattered to be asked. It's been fantastic to work with you and your team. Thank you for your help and support the whole way through, and it was great to meet you in person at the London Book Fair.

Thank you to my amazing tech editor Rachel Vowles – she's my rock! She spends hours ensuring that all the patterns are correct, making the charts and drawing up the schematics. She works with me on most of my designs and I just couldn't do it without her. It's been fantastic to work on such a big project with her by my side every step of the way.

Another huge thank-you goes out to Scheepjes, who supplied all the lovely yarn for the projects. I really enjoy working with these yarns so was honoured when Scheepjes said they would be happy for me to use them in the book. Also to Wool Warehouse who supplied yarn for the one of the projects in the book, special mention to Gill Bailey.

And then there are Marie Barley and Su Smith who have helped photograph some of the projects – and me! – here in the UK. I'm eternally grateful to you both for giving up your time to help me achieve this book.

A heartfelt thank-you goes out to my partner, Cliff, whose motto in life is "Anything is possible". Thank you for supporting me through the writing of this book, it is you who you have shown me through your own hard work and determination that you can achieve anything. Sorry for leaving bits of wool all over your sofa.

Thank you to my other male role model: my dad. He's the unsung hero in my life, really. Thank you for being my biggest fan and for supporting me both emotionally and financially whilst I focus on being an independent woman!

Last but by no means least, thank you to my two favorite people, Harvey and Alfie, my beautiful twins. I gave you life but you two have taught me so much about life, through your grit and dedication to be successful and win at whatever you do. Thank you for putting up with balls of wool everywhere, a really messy house and few takeaway teas. I hope I've shown you that us three, our little team, we really can do anything we put our minds to.

Cassie